THE *QUEEN OF THE NORTH* DISASTER

THE QUEEN OF THE NORTH DISASTER

The Captain's Story

Colin Henthorne

HARBOUR
PUBLISHING

HARBOUR PUBLISHING CO. LTD.

PO Box 219, Madeira Park, BC, VON 2H0
www.harbourpublishing.com

Edited by Audrey McClellan
Indexed by Kyla Shauer
Printed and bound in Canada
Printed on acid-free,
FSC-certified stock

Back cover photo by
Jim Thorne/Wett Coast/Flickr
Cover design by
Anna Comfort O'Keeffe
Text design by Shed Simas

Harbour Publishing acknowledges the support of the Canada Council for the Arts, which last year invested $153 million to bring the arts to Canadians throughout the country. We also gratefully acknowledge financial support from the Government of Canada through the Canada Book Fund and from the Province of British Columbia through the BC Arts Council and the Book Publishing Tax Credit.

LIBRARY AND ARCHIVES CANADA CATALOGUING IN PUBLICATION

Henthorne, Colin, author
    The Queen of the North disaster : the captain's story / Colin Henthorne.

Includes bibliographical references and index.
Issued in print and electronic formats.
ISBN 978-1-55017-761-9 (paperback).--ISBN 978-1-55017-724-4 (html)

1. Queen of the North (Ferry). 2. Shipwrecks--British Columbia.
3. Shipwrecks--Inside Passage. 4. Ferries--Accidents--British Columbia.
5. Ferries--Accidents--Inside Passage. I. Title.

G530.Q45H45 2016   910.9164'33   C2016-905444-6
                                               C2016-905445-4

This book is dedicated to the memory of my parents and the memory of Howard Ehrlich, to my family, friends, and shipmates, and to all who have stood by me.

You can't, in sound morals, condemn a man for taking care of his own integrity. It is his clear duty.

—Joseph Conrad, *A Personal Record*

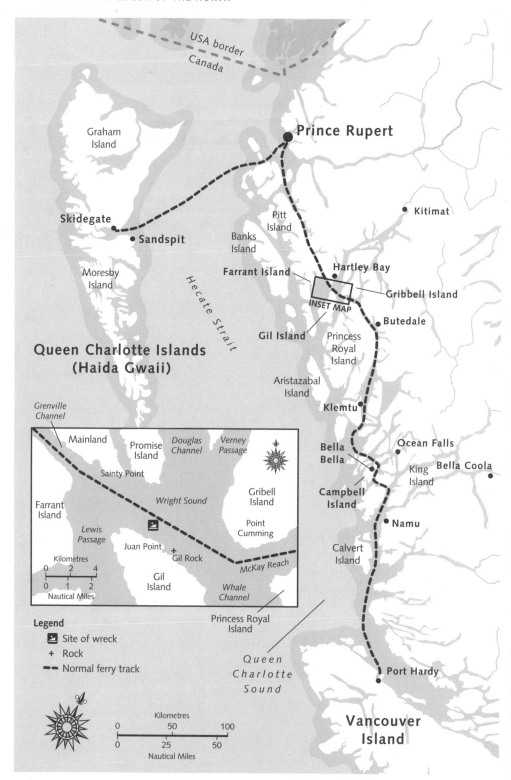

USA border
Canada

Prince Rupert

Graham
Island

Kitimat

Pitt
Island

Skidegate

Banks
Island

Sandspit

Farrant Island

Hartley Bay

Moresby
Island

Gribbell Island

Hecate Strait

Gil Island

Princess
Royal
Island

Butedale

Queen Charlotte Islands
(Haida Gwaii)

Aristazabal
Island

Klemtu

Grenville
Channel

Mainland

Promise
Island

Douglas
Channel

Verney
Passage

**Bella
Bella**

Ocean Falls

Sainty Point

Gribell
Island

King
Island

Bella Coola

Farrant
Island

Wright Sound

Point
Cumming

**Campbell
Island**

Lewis
Passage

Juan Point

Gil Rock

Namu

Kilometres

0   2   4

0   1   2

Nautical Miles

Gil
Island

McKay Reach

Whale
Channel

Calvert
Island

Princess Royal
Island

Legend

⛴ Site of wreck

+ Rock

‑ ‑ Normal ferry track

Queen
Charlotte
Sound

Port Hardy

Kilometres

0   50   100

0   25   50

Nautical Miles

Vancouver
Island

CONTENTS

LIST OF ABBREVIATIONS

2/O   second officer or second mate

4/O   fourth officer or fourth mate

ABS   American Bureau of Shipping

ARPA   Automatic Radar Plotting Aid (a computer attached to the radar)

BHP   brake horsepower

BRM   Bridge Resource Management (a maritime version of aviation's Cockpit Resource Management or Crew Resource Management)

CPP   controllable pitch propeller

CRM   Cockpit Resource Management; later changed to Crew Resource Management

DI   Divisional Inquiry

ECS   electronic chart system

ETA   expected time of arrival

FRC   Fast Response Craft

GPS   Global Positioning System (satellite-based navigation system that can be integrated with the electronic chart system)

IMO   International Maritime Organization

ISM   International Safety Management Code (international standard for the safe management and operation of ships and for pollution prevention)

JRCC   Joint Rescue Co-ordination Centre (JRCC Victoria is one of three centres in Canada and is responsible for Air-Sea Rescue in British Columbia, the Yukon, and up to 550 nautical miles/1,000 kilometres offshore in the Pacific)

MCTS   Marine Communications and Traffic Services (Canadian Coast Guard service that provides vessel traffic services and waterway management, broadcasts weather and safety information, and co-ordinates marine safety communications with the Joint Rescue Co-ordination Centre)

NASA   National Aeronautics and Space Administration (US)

NTSB   National Transportation Safety Board (US)

OOW   officer of the watch

OSC   on-scene co-ordinator

QM   quartermaster

QM1   Quartermaster Karen Briker (term used in the Transportation Safety Board's report on the sinking of the *Queen of the North*)

QN   *Queen of the North*

SEN   Simulated Electronic Navigation (training in the use of electronic navigation systems and instruments; includes computer simulations)

SOLAS   International Convention for Safety of Life at Sea

TSB   Transportation Safety Board

VDR   Voyage Data Recorder

VHF   Very High Frequency

WCAT   Workers' Compensation Appeal Tribunal (a body that hears appeals of Workers' Compensation Board decisions)

WCB   Workers' Compensation Board (AKA WorkSafeBC)

NOTE TO READERS

JUST AFTER MIDNIGHT ON MARCH 22, 2006, THE PASSENGER SHIP the *Queen of the North* struck an underwater ledge on the Gil Island shore of Wright Sound on the British Columbia coast. Unlike most ships that have gone aground, she did not stay aground. Striking the ledge at a speed of 17.5 knots, she ran clear across it, tearing holes in the ship's bottom and along the starboard side, and ripping out the propellers. Her momentum carried her on into deep water, where no force on earth could keep her afloat. In just over an hour she sank to the bottom of Wright Sound, 1,400 feet (427 metres) below the surface.

In contrast to most sinkings, the ship was evacuated with no outside assistance. Two passengers went missing and remain missing to this day.

The sinking of the *Queen of the North* was one of the top news stories in Canada for 2006. I was the captain. This is my story.

CHAPTER 1

FLAGSHIP

UNTIL THE INCIDENT DESCRIBED IN THIS BOOK, I WAS WHAT COULD safely be called a career mariner. I got off to an early start. As we were growing up on the water, my father taught my brothers and me to handle boats under oars, sails, and power. He also taught us how to build, maintain, and repair boats. More formal training came my way as a sea cadet from age twelve to eighteen. By the time I was twenty-one I had my first command, an 80-foot (24-metre) training vessel. I worked for various outfits after that, towing logs and operating other small coastal craft. At age twenty-two I joined the Coast Guard and spent eight years there, starting as a deckhand before becoming a seaman/diver, then a first mate, and, ultimately, captain. After leaving the Coast Guard I worked in the petroleum industry, serving in two different offshore exploration vessels and two different icebreakers in the Arctic. Along the way I did such things as operating a hovercraft at the Expo site in Vancouver, working as mate and master on tugboats towing barges on the British Columbia coast and up the Fraser and Pitt Rivers, and spending some time with the Department of Fisheries.

In 1987 I was looking for something steadier, with opportunity for advancement, so I applied for a job with the biggest employer in coastal waters, BC Ferries. To get on with them I had to go back to being a deckhand, working on a casual basis and accumulating seniority. Except for a short stint working out of Tsawwassen, I worked in BC Ferries' Northern Service on the *Queen of Prince Rupert* and the *Queen of the North*, sailing most of the time as a master, although my regular position was first mate.

Eventually I became a full-time master with what is known as exempt status, but it took nineteen years.

BC FERRIES

British Columbia comprises some 357,000 square miles (925,000 square kilometres) of dry land, but 70 percent of its population occupies a narrow zone where the land meets the Pacific Ocean. The coast is a myriad of inlets and islands, producing one of the world's most intricate inshore waterways. This has resulted in a heavy dependence on watercraft from the time aboriginal peoples plied the coast in dugout canoes to the days of the fondly remembered steamship companies that enabled European settlement.

The coast was a likely spot for the growth of one of the world's great ferry companies, the seed for which was planted in 1923 when Canadian Pacific built what is believed to be the first "roll-on/roll-off" automobile ferry, the *Motor Princess*. In 1958, when a strike shut down both the Black Ball Ferry Company and the Canadian Pacific Steamship Service, the two ferry operators on which Vancouver Island had become dependent, the Social Credit government of the time decided to form a publicly owned ferry service, the British Columbia Ferry Authority, in response. Reorganized and renamed numerous times over the years, the fleet has generally been known simply as BC Ferries.

The first terminals built by BC Ferries were at Tsawwassen, south of Vancouver, and Swartz Bay, north of Victoria, and two ships were put into service by 1960. These early vessels were highly efficient traffic movers; this, combined with the fact that cargo was being moved more and more by truck rather than barge, led to increased demand for ferry service. By 1965, seven more ships had been launched, and soon some were being modified to accommodate more vehicles and passengers. BC Ferries also purchased vessels from various commercial operators, including the above-mentioned *Motor Princess*, which was renamed *Pender Queen*. In the 1970s and early 1980s the corporation ordered several much larger vessels, the 449-foot (137-metre) "C" Class ferries, which were the largest double-ended ships in the world at that time. Growth continued with the acquisition of two 548-foot (167-metre) Spirit Class vessels in 1993, followed by three 525-foot (160-metre) German-built Super C ferries in 2007. Initially a branch of the Ministry of Highways, BC Ferries became a Crown corporation in 1977, and in 2003 was reorganized along the lines of a private company, although it remains publicly owned and is securely bound to the Government of British Columbia by a services contract.[1] In 2014–15, the company ran thirty-four vessels on twenty-four routes to forty-seven terminals, carrying 19.8 million passengers and 7.7 million vehicles throughout coastal British Columbia, making it one of the largest ferry systems in the world.[2]

BC Ferries' Northern Service, based in Prince Rupert and serving the upper BC coast as far north as Prince Rupert and the Queen Charlotte Islands (since renamed Haida Gwaii), began operations in 1966 with the new Victoria-built *Queen of Prince Rupert*, which at first used Kelsey Bay for its southern terminus. When the Island Highway was extended to Port Hardy in 1979, the terminal moved to that community. The 270-nautical mile[3] (500-kilometre) route BC Ferries established through the Inside Passage is by far the longest and most challenging in the company's system. By 1980, the *Queen of Prince Rupert* was in need of backup on the northern run, and this was when the *Queen of the North* entered the Northern Service as the year-round vessel. In the late 1990s, the two ships exchanged roles, with the *Queen of Prince Rupert* working year-round, and the *Queen of the North* providing extra capacity during peak season and relieving while the *Queen of Prince Rupert* was in refit, which is what she was doing on March 22, 2006.

THE *QUEEN OF THE NORTH*

The *Queen of the North* was built in Bremerhaven, Germany, in 1969 for the Stena Line of Sweden. They named her *Stena Danica*. For five years

• • • • • • • • • • • •

1   "About BC Ferries," on the BC Ferry Commission website, http://www.bcferry commission.ca/faqs/about-bc-ferries/ and "About BC Ferries: Our Company," on the BC Ferries website, http://www.bcferries.com/about/More_Information.html

2   British Columbia Ferry Services Inc. and BC Ferry Authority, *Annual Report 2014–2015* (Victoria: Author, 2015), 2.

3   Throughout this book, "mile" means "nautical mile." The British Standard Nautical Mile is 6,080 feet (1,853.18 metres); the International Nautical Mile is 6,076.10 feet (1,852 metres).

she carried passengers and cars between Frederikshavn, Denmark, and Gothenburg, Sweden. In 1974 Stena sold her to the BC Ferry Corporation, which put her to work between Horseshoe Bay on the mainland and Departure Bay on Vancouver Island, a distance of 30 nautical miles (56 kilometres). She was on that run only until 1975.[4] Her turnaround times were too long and her car-carrying capacity was less than half that of the smaller, purpose-built ferries. She was laid up in Deas Dock until she found her calling on the northern run. (For the *Queen of the North*'s specifications, please see Appendix F.)

Although she was commonly called a "ferry," the proper term for her was "passenger ship." A ferry is a vessel for transporting people or vehicles across a short stretch, such as a river, lake, harbour, or strait. The *Queen of the North* was built for and used for transporting people and cars over much greater distances and in exposed waters. The distance from Prince Rupert to Skidegate, on Graham Island, is 100 nautical miles (185 kilometres) and involves crossing Hecate Strait, a body of water whose severe sea conditions compare to those of the central North Sea.[5] The trip from Prince Rupert to Port Hardy, on Vancouver Island, also exposes ships to the open ocean as they cross Milbanke Sound and then Queen Charlotte Sound.

Because of the nature of her business, the *Queen of the North* looked nothing like a typical ferry. Her profile was that of an ocean-going ship, and she was often mistaken for a cruise ship. The architects had cleverly disguised her car-carrying role by designing her bow in such a way that it opened up like the visor on a knight's helmet; in fact, this portion of the bow was termed the "visor." When opened, it revealed another medieval but practical device: a drawbridge (called the "ramp") that lowered onto the shore bridge to load and unload vehicles.

She was a beautiful ship. Like all beautiful ships, her visual beauty was matched by her practicality. In fact, those two elements were intertwined. Viewed from above, her shape was a slender ellipse, perfectly adapted to

· · · · · · · · · · · ·

4   I travelled aboard her in 1975 on my way to Canadian Forces Base Comox, where I was stationed in command of a naval training vessel. I never imagined that sixteen years later I would be captain of this beautiful ship.

5   Canadian Hydrographic Service, *Sailing Directions: General Information—Pacific Coast*, 2nd ed. (Ottawa: Minister of Fisheries and Oceans Canada, 2006), 5-25.

the sea. Her flared bow, with its concave curves, was an elegant feature that acted as one big shock absorber, a true hydraulic damper that enabled her to go to sea in rough weather. It reduced the degree to which the ship would pitch in heavy seas, and it reduced the violence of that pitching to something resembling comfort.

The most important part of any ship is the part you cannot see: the underwater portion of the hull. The *Queen of the North*'s hull was rounded, carefully constructed to increase her stability and efficiency. Her draft (the depth of the ship below the waterline) was a little more than 17 feet (5 metres). The underwater portion of her bow was bulbous, to reduce the drag caused by its wave. Similarly, her rounded stern made her much easier to steer in a following sea than would have been the case with a square stern. Strong headwinds noticeably reduced her speed but somewhat less than they would have done if she had not been streamlined above the waterline as well.

Two enormous underwater wings—the stabilizers—protruded from the bilges (the rounded parts of the hull where the bottom meets the sides). These stabilizers were gyro-controlled and hydraulically activated. They reacted continuously to ship movement caused by waves and wind, thereby limiting both the degree and the speed of the roll, changing it from violent to gentle. When not required, they retracted into the hull.

Stability and seaworthiness are necessary for any ship. The *Queen of the North* had another very desirable characteristic: she was "sea kindly," which means that although she pitched and rolled, as does every vessel, these motions were not so abrupt. Except in the worst of weather, she rode quite comfortably. Even the streamlining of the upper superstructure (Decks 5 and 6) and houseworks (Decks 7 and 8) contributed to maintaining her speed with efficiency.

The *Queen of the North* had a double bottom, as do all large ships except for older tankers. The space between the inner and outer bottoms was occupied by the framework. Although this framework could be described as cellular, technically this type of construction is termed a "transverse framing system."[6] The main frames ran transversely across the ship and continued up the sides. These are the "ribs" of a ship. For continuity of

. . . .

6   The other commonly used system in shipbuilding is the longitudinal or Isherwood framing system. In that system the longitudinal frames are the heavier.

QUEEN OF THE NORTH INBOARD PROFILE

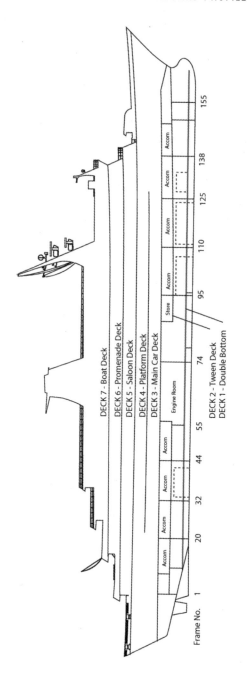

DECK 7 - Boat Deck
DECK 6 - Promenade Deck
DECK 5 - Saloon Deck
DECK 4 - Platform Deck
DECK 3 - Main Car Deck
DECK 2 - Tween Deck
DECK 1 - Double Bottom

Engine Room

Accom Accom Accom Accom Accom Accom Accom Accom Store Accom

Frame No. 1   20   32   44   55   74   95   110   125   138   155

R. N. Pearson illustration

strength, each of the transverse bulkheads in the ship was directly above a transverse frame. There were eleven of these watertight bulkheads on Deck 1, where the engine rooms were located, and another six bulkheads on Deck 2. These bulkheads divided the ship into separate compartments and so would restrict the spread of flooding if any compartment was holed. The *Queen of the North* was designed to stay afloat if one compartment flooded, and for this reason architects described her as a "one-compartment" ship. The term tends to cause confusion because it sounds as if the ship only had one compartment. She had multiple compartments but would only survive the flooding of one.

The heart of the ship, the two engine rooms, was approximately amidships on Deck 1. One engine room housed the main engines (for propulsion); the other was the generator room. The main engines comprised two sixteen-cylinder diesels from Maschinenfabrik Augsburg-Nürnberg mechanical engineering company of Germany, each producing 7,800 brake horsepower (BHP) for a total of 15,600 BHP. Maximum RPM was 360, about half the speed of a car engine's idle. No clutch, no gearbox; each engine was coupled directly to a long propeller shaft. These twin propeller shafts were spaced 20 feet (6 metres) apart, and each led to a controllable pitch propeller, 9 feet (2.7 metres) in diameter. A spade-shaped rudder was located directly behind each propeller. Top speed was better than 22 knots. Adjacent to the main engine room (Deck 1) was a well-equipped workshop with a metal-turning lathe and a drill press.

Next to the lifesaving equipment, the most important pieces of equipment in a ship are the generators. The *Queen of the North* had three Caterpillar diesel-powered generators, each producing 400 kilowatts. In a small room on Deck 8 was the emergency generator, a Volvo Penta producing 150 kilowatts. Above Deck 8, the enormous, high funnel kept the exhaust gases and occasional soot from the engines away from the air intakes and the decks.

Deck 5 was the uppermost continuous deck—that is, it ran the full length of the ship.[7] It included a good-sized, open foredeck (not a true forecastle, which would have been a raised deck). On the foredeck were the two anchor windlasses (winches), which incorporated the line-handling

· · · · · · · · · · · ·

7   The decks are numbered from the bottom to the top. Deck 1, technically, is not a deck but the upper plates of the double bottom—it is properly referred to as the "tank top."

winches, used when the ship was to be made fast in dock. These were called "tension winches" because they automatically kept the lines at a predetermined tension. Each windlass controlled its own 2.5-ton (2.3-tonne) anchor and nine shackles (810 feet/247 metres) of 1.25-inch (31.75-millimetre) special steel-studded chain.

The navigating bridge was at the forward end of Deck 7. It incorporated the wheelhouse, which was the largest section and housed navigational instrumentation as well as the steering wheels, the chartroom, and the radio room. Up until 1989, the *Queen of the North* and the *Queen of Prince Rupert* carried radio operators; Morse code, as well as voice communication, was used regularly.[8] By 2006, most of the old radio equipment had been removed.

In the wheelhouse were the steering and propulsion controls and the navigation instruments and aids, including three radars, GPS,[9] an electronic chart system (ECS), paper charts, publications, a Doppler speed log (which indicates the ship's speed through the water), a gyro compass, and two echo sounders capable of measuring the depth of water below the ship at three different points along the keel. To keep the magnetic compass as free as possible from the magnetic interference produced by an all-steel ship, it was mounted above the wheelhouse; a periscope arrangement was provided so it could be read in the wheelhouse by the helmsman and the navigator.

Also located in this "nerve centre" were the controls for the watertight doors on Decks 1 and 2 and the fire doors throughout the ship, switches for navigation lights, the general alarm and fire alarm, plus myriad other

. . . .

8   This fact is often greeted with derision by those who find such things as Morse code to be anachronistic. In fact, there are many advantages to Morse code. There is practically no language barrier, and no difficult accents or voices to try to understand. The low-frequency signal can travel great distances, and there is no line-of-sight restriction, so it is not affected much by topography, which affects even satellite communications. On October 4, 1980, the passenger ship *Prinsendam*, overcome by fire, sent out an SOS in Morse code. Thanks to that signal—and the search-and-rescue crews of the Royal Canadian Air Force and the US Coast Guard—all 535 people on board were saved.

9   Global Positioning System, a satellite-based navigation system, is one of two Global Navigation Satellite Systems in operation. The other is the Russian GLONASS (roughly, an acronym of the Russian version of Global Navigation Satellite System).

QUEEN OF THE NORTH BRIDGE LAYOUT

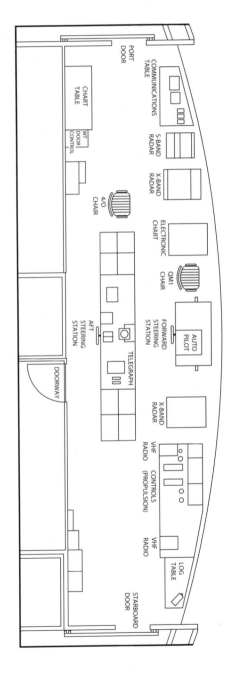

Mark Temple illustration

mundane switches and controls for such things as windshield wipers and defrosters.

The bridge's outer extensions or "wings" ran out past the sides of the superstructure. We had to pass through a door and go outside to access them. They were open, unprotected from the weather. On each wing was a grating of teak. Standing upon it, the captain had at hand a control bench with engine controls, instrumentation, and searchlights, so the ship could be handled from the wings when docking or manoeuvring at close quarters.

The wheelhouse contained a mix of old and new equipment. I have always had difficulty using the word "layout" when describing it. To me, "layout" suggests something that is planned. I am more inclined to describe the arrangement of the *Queen of the North*'s bridge as haphazard. The word "ergonomic" was not part of the maritime lexicon in 1969, and to this day very few people involved in shipbuilding and design seem to understand the concept. Ultimately, I believe this absence of any ergonomic planning contributed to my ship's demise.

One feature that affected the arrangement of bridge equipment was the bow visor, mentioned earlier. With the visor raised for a bow-on docking, the view ahead was blocked. It was like trying to drive a car into a garage with the car's hood up. To compensate for this, the propulsion controls—normally located on a ship's centre-line—were off to one side. The steering wheel, however, was on the ship's centre-line and on an island workbench (or console). The helmsman stood with hands on the wheel and back against the after bulkhead (the "back wall") of the wheelhouse. At the forward bulkhead, and on the centre-line, was the forward steering unit, which housed the gyro compass and the automatic pilot. It is important to understand that the automatic pilot, despite its name, does not pilot or navigate the ship. All it does is steer the ship along a set course. If an obstacle happens to be situated on that course, the autopilot will blithely run the ship right into it. Controls for the forward steering unit were divided into two groups: some were on the unit itself, while others were on the island workbench directly in front of the helmsman's position.

Significant distances and one large obstacle separated these three vital control stations: the aft steering station, the forward steering station, and the propulsion control station.

It was never convenient. On March 22, 2006, I believe it contributed to the loss of the ship.

Out the after door of the wheelhouse was the chartroom, and through the side door of the chartroom was a corridor called an "alley" or "alleyway." Across the alley was the old radio room. If you walked down the alley toward the stern, you passed rooms, or "cabins," on either side. These were the accommodations for the officers (the captain, the mates, the engineers, and the chief and second stewards). It was while walking down this alleyway one day that I realized I had spent more time in this ship than I had in any home I'd ever lived in. No wonder it was so familiar to me.

My cabin was the second door on the starboard side. By the standards of 1969, when the ship was built, this accommodation was opulent. It was definitely bigger and better than any ship's cabin I had ever had before. It contained a fairly large "day room," which was my living room/office, as well as a small bedroom with a single bunk, and a bathroom with shower.

The day room was fitted out with comfortable chairs and a sofa, sideboards with bookcases, a television set that received satellite stations, a stereo, my desk and chair, a small fridge, and—under a tablecloth that disguised it as a side table—the master's safe. Two telephones connected me to every part of the ship. Prints of Emily Carr paintings decorated the room, and a few personal possessions gave it an individual touch. The result was a comfortable home, well-suited for duty and relaxation alike.

When I was ashore, I lived near Calgary, Alberta. This struck a lot of people as a rather strange location for a West Coast mariner to live, but the work schedule on live-aboard ships allows one to live practically anywhere. Traditionally, BC Ferries' casual employees on ships based in Prince Rupert lived locally, but most regular employees lived on the Lower Mainland of British Columbia or on Vancouver Island, making a commute once every two weeks. Gradually, more and more employees took up homes in the interior of British Columbia, and three of our able seamen lived in Alberta or Saskatchewan. When I discovered that I could commute just as cheaply and easily from Calgary as from Vancouver, we sold our home in Tsawwassen and bought an acreage south of Calgary. I loved the wide open space, the blue skies, and my view of the Rocky Mountains. I was born and raised in British Columbia, and my family's roots are deep there, but they are also wide. I was no stranger to Wild Rose Country, having spent many a childhood holiday there, "helping" my uncles, aunts, and cousins with their farming and ranching. Calgary was also much closer to Nelson, BC, the home of my parents.

On the *Queen of the North*, generally, and with some anomalies, the sizes of the cabins decreased with rank. For members of the crew who were not in the officer class, cabins were below the waterline and small. Almost all of those were fitted with two bunks. Some crew were accommodated two to a cabin, others had cabins to themselves.

The deck below the bridge and my cabin, Deck 6, was divided into three sections. The Forward Section, which was a large seating area with reclining seats, was the Prince of Wales Lounge, named in 1986 when the *Queen of the North* carried the Prince and Princess of Wales, Charles and Diana, for their visit to Expo 86, the World's Fair at Vancouver. A large framed poster hung in the lounge to commemorate the event. Over the years, the lounge had featured a liquor bar and a coffee bar, but in 2006 it offered no refreshments, though there were several television sets, used for playing movies.

The Midships (middle) Section of Deck 6 was another large seating area with reclining seats and a children's playroom, while the Aft Section contained passenger cabins.

Deck 5 had a large cafeteria in the after section, and a buffet and lounge in the forward section. Midships was the galley, the purser's office, and the elevator.

Decks 3 and 4 were the car decks, though Deck 4 was merely a droppable platform offering extra space for cars.

Deck 2, below the waterline, was called the Tween Deck, as it was between the car deck and the double bottom (tank top). It housed crew quarters aft and obsolete passenger cabins forward. There was no midships section to this deck as the engine room towered through it from Deck 1.

THE RUNNING OF THE SHIP

The popular image of a ship's captain has a man holding the spokes of a ship's steering wheel, sporting a peaked cap and a beard. The reality is very different. Although most, but not all, captains are men, and there are a few captains with beards, very few own a peaked cap, and none of them steer their ships.

Ships are steered by "helmsmen." These are able seamen or ordinary seamen who have been specially trained for the duty. The name derives from "helm," a term that encompasses every type of steering device: wheel, tiller, steering oar, automatic pilot, etc. People often use the phrase "at the helm" metaphorically to mean any person in charge of something—such as the president of a corporation—but it is inaccurate to describe the captain of a ship as the person who directly steers the vessel.

In some ships, helmsmen are generally referred to as "deckhands"—and their duties almost invariably include general deck duties—but they are more properly termed "quartermasters." The origins of the word are unclear, but one plausible explanation traces its derivation to the same source as quarterdeck—originally a deck that comprised one-quarter the length of the ship, but which is now only the stern part of the ship. Large sailing ships were steered, navigated, and commanded from the quarterdeck. The man who ruled this part of the ship (under the captain or master) was the quartermaster. The use of the term has varied over the centuries. As they say, "different ships, different long splices," meaning that there is more than one correct way to perform any job. In the *Queen of the North*, we used the term "quartermaster" to acknowledge that the specialized duties of this person included lookout duties and security duties, such as fire and security patrols or "rounds," as well as steering. Also, when the ship is being steered by the automatic pilot, it is the quartermaster who controls the automatic pilot.

Steering is only one part of navigation. We never say that the helmsman is navigating. That duty is taken on by mates and, occasionally, by the master.

A ship under way—meaning that it is not at anchor or secured to the shore—is "under the conduct" of a suitably qualified mariner. The qualifications vary according to the size and type of the vessel, its voyage classification, and whether it is in a compulsory pilotage area. Voyage classification is determined by the length of the voyage and whether the waters are sheltered, partially sheltered, or not sheltered. A compulsory pilotage area is an area where the Pilotage Regulations require the ship to be under the conduct of a licensed pilot, a person who is not part of the crew. A pilot licence is valid for a certain area or areas of the coast. The *Queen of the North* operated mostly in compulsory pilotage areas, but under the Pilotage Regulations of the time was exempted from the requirement that a licensed pilot be aboard because it was a domestic vessel and the crew was familiar with the area. Had it been a foreign vessel, a pilot would have been compulsory.

The *Queen of the North* was required by regulation to carry a master, a first mate, and a second mate. Under company policy, we also carried two additional crew with the minimum of a second mate's certificate, filling the positions of third mate and fourth mate. The master and all four mates were each fully qualified to have the conduct of the ship throughout its area of operations.

At all times there were four quartermasters on duty and two mates. Of the two mates on duty, one—either the first or second mate—was the "Senior"; the other—either the third or fourth mate—was the "Junior."

When the ship was under way, the bridge at all times had a minimum of one quartermaster, who was on the helm, and one mate, who had the conduct of the ship and was designated the "Officer of the Watch" (oow).

In most ships, only one mate is on duty at any one time. BC Ferries instituted the system of having two mates on duty so that they could share the workload on the bridge when that load is heaviest—specifically, during times of restricted visibility and through the more challenging passages. This also allows one of the mates to attend to a wide variety of matters that take place off the bridge, security and safety issues in particular. It was left to the senior mate to decide when and if one of the mates would leave the bridge. However, it was normal for both mates to spend most of their time on the bridge. Meals were taken as work allowed.

The four quartermasters worked a rotation of one hour on the wheel, one hour on fire and security patrols, one hour on car deck patrol, and one hour on general duties. As with the mates, they fit meals in as the work allowed.

The person who has the conduct of the ship is in charge of the navigation, which includes planning, monitoring, and conducting the passage of the ship from one place to another. Navigation of the ship also encompasses full control of course, speed, and the use of helm, engines, and any other controls such as the thrusters.

The conduct of the ship is not shared. It can be held by the senior mate or the junior mate but not both, and it can be held by the master. When the junior mate has the conduct of the ship, the senior mate is the supervisor and may give the junior direction. The senior mate may also take over the conduct, but it is always clear that the conduct is held by one person only, and it is always clearly established which person that is. The captain is the supervisor of the entire crew and may give direction or order that the conduct be given to one person in particular. The captain may also take over the conduct.

The master's presence on the bridge is a matter for the individual master's discretion and preferences. At a minimum, masters will be on the bridge for entering and leaving harbour, during times of restricted visibility, and during those passages which require the greatest attention. Additionally, most masters will be on the bridge from time to time to monitor the performance of the ship and the crew. As a principle of leadership, masters never justify to anyone their reasons for being on the bridge or for taking over the conduct of the ship. Sometimes it is done to set an example, sometimes it is to keep one's skills current, and sometimes the master just feels that it is for the best.

Seamen have always been generalists. Ship owners invariably want to keep crew size small in order to maximize profit, but even with the most generous of owners, practicality dictates that seamen will always do what needs to be done. At one time, the ships in the Northern Service of BC Ferries carried thirteen able seamen. Sometime before 1988, when I joined the Northern Service, the number was reduced to eight. Therefore, when the quartermasters and mates are not engaged in their duties of navigation and security, they are required to perform the tasks of loading the car deck, cleaning ship (quartermasters), and taking care of general maintenance and seamanship duties. So when people remark that the running of a ship through the treacherous waters of the British Columbia coast is left to "deckhands," they are mistaken. It is more accurate to say that the skilled and well-qualified professionals who operate the ship are also saddled with the non-navigational tasks of the deckhand.

The *Queen of the North*, like the *Queen of Prince Rupert*, had two complete crews—"A" crew and "B" crew—on a two-weeks-on/two-weeks-off rotation, with each crew member working a twelve-hour day and living on board for the duration of the two weeks.[10] Because the *Queen of the North* operated around the clock, seven days a week, the crew complement needed to be large enough to cover a twenty-four-hour period, and the crew needed to work in shifts. Shifts aboard ship have always been termed "watches."

The twelve-hour workday provided full coverage and at the same time

. . . .

10   BC Ferries uses the word "watch" in place of "crew." This is because almost all its vessels operate on short runs, and the crews go home at the end of their watches. In all but the three vessels that have live-aboard crews, the entire crew is changed at the end of the watch. In the case of the live-aboard ships, the habit of using the term "watch" in place of "crew" has carried over, but it is improper. I have tried to stick with the term "crew" throughout this book.

was beneficial for both the employee and the employer. The employees benefited from two weeks off after two weeks of work because they had worked 168 hours, an average of forty-two hours per week over the full four-week period. The employer benefited by being able to keep the crew size to a minimum.

Various arrangements have been tried over the years to find the ideal watch schedule on board: a straight twelve-hour watch is one option, as are watches of six hours on/six hours off, or a variety or eight and four or nine and three splits. When I first joined the Northern Service in 1988, we worked an eight and four split. Then we tried a nine and three split for a time, and eventually we settled on the straight twelve.

When the *Queen of the North* sailed from Prince Rupert on the evening of March 21, 2006, the deck watch system looked like this:

DAY WATCH	NIGHT WATCH
0600–1800 (6 a.m. to 6 p.m.)	1800–0600 (6 p.m. to 6 a.m.)
First Mate: Richard St. Pierre	Second Mate: Keven Hilton
Third Mate: Shiney O'Neill	Fourth Mate: Karl Lilgert
Four Quartermasters:	Four Quartermasters:
Dave Baker	Karen Briker
Jim Hansen	Rob Burn
Ryan Johnson	Don Gordon
Roy Spletzer	Jason Laporte

The exact makeup of the crew was constantly changing due to the nature of the business. Throughout a two-week shift, there would usually be some partial change in crew just about every time the ship docked in its home port. For example, Karen Briker, one of the quartermasters on March 21, had gone home on sick leave on March 17 but rejoined the vessel on March 20 and immediately began working a twelve-hour night shift.[11] The number of crew also varied between forty and sixty-five, depending on the season and on the number of passengers to be carried. In the past, BC Ferries did

. . . .

11   Transportation Safety Board, "Striking and Subsequent Sinking: Passenger and Vehicle Ferry *Queen of the North*, Gil Island, Wright Sound, British Columbia, 22 March 2006," Marine Investigation Report M06W0052 (http://www.tsb.gc.ca/eng/rapports -reports/marine/2006/m06w0052/m06w0052.asp), 25 (hereafter TSB Report).

what most transportation companies did and kept full-time employees on standby. That practice was discontinued over thirty years ago. The result is a cadre of casual employees that has been growing exponentially.

Crewing was carried out by the office ashore in Prince Rupert, which decided who would fill what position, on what shift, and on what watch. The crewing office worked within some pretty tight constraints. Out of fairness, an attempt was made to keep most regular crew alternating between day watch and night watch, so that a regular employee would work two weeks of day watches, take two weeks off, and return for two weeks of night watches. There were, however, numerous complications: people were off sick, others went on courses or on vacation, casual employees as well as regulars could achieve their maximum number of hours in a month prematurely, etc. In nearly all cases, when a casual crew member came aboard, it was to fill a specific vacancy. That meant it was very clear which watch that person would be standing. Although the master or a department head could and would make or request changes if they had strong reasons, the composition and watch schedule of the crew was pretty much fixed.

THE *QUEEN'S* ROUTE

As mentioned, the *Queen of the North* travelled regularly between Skidegate and Prince Rupert, and Prince Rupert and Port Hardy. The latter journey took her through what is known as the Inside Passage, a network of channels providing almost continuous shelter for the entire length of the BC coast. Ships on this route are exposed to the open ocean in two places: Milbanke Sound and Queen Charlotte Sound. Aside from them, the widest part of the passage is Wright Sound, where the width is 2.2 nautical miles (4 kilometres). For the most part, the channels are narrow, the narrowest being a section of Grenville Channel, which constricts to a width of 250 yards (228 metres) at Ormiston Point. Grenville Channel is 46 miles (85 kilometres) long. When foreign passengers travelled with us, they sometimes wondered if the ship had entered a river.

To understand the nature of the BC coast, picture a mountain range that has been flooded to leave the mountains only half exposed. In many places the sides of the channel are sheer cliffs, and the water is deep enough that a large ship can actually lie alongside them. Depths as great as 418 fathoms (2,500 feet/765 metres) are found along the route.

Because the Inside Passage is so narrow, with so many turns, naviga-tors make more than seventy alterations of course between Prince Rupert and Port Hardy.

It was a tricky route, but even though I was not sailing with my regular crew (I was usually with "A" crew, but due to a staffing anomaly I was tem-porarily placed on "B" crew and had been with them for one week), I was not concerned. The competency of all mates and engineers is certified by the Minister of Transport, every crew member is required to go through a familiarization process for both the ship and the route, and a record of their employment and qualifications is available on board for the master to review. The four mates—the navigators—each had over 10,000 hours' experience. Keven Hilton, the second mate, for example, had been with BC Ferries for about twenty-five years, obtaining his watchkeeping mate, ship certificate in 1997 and his first mate, intermediate voyage certificate in 2001. Fourth mate Karl Lilgert had worked on fishing boats before joining BC Ferries in 1990. He had obtained his watchkeeping mate certificate and Simulated Electronic Navigation (SEN-I) training in 1995, and his certificate of competency to serve in the capacity of an officer in charge of a navigational watch for near coastal voyages in 2002.[12]

THE MASTER

In February 2006, I accepted an offer from BC Ferries to become an ex-cluded master. For sixteen years I had been sailing as master in the *Queen of the North* and the *Queen of Prince Rupert*. However, my official position was chief officer (first mate). Technically, I was only substituting into the position of master, and I spent roughly 25 to 30 percent of each year sailing as first mate.

The move from chief officer to master was not a straightforward pro-motion. Long before I came to the company, BC Ferries had succeeded in getting its ships' masters declared "management" and removed from union representation. They came to be known as "excluded masters" and, more recently, "exempt masters." When these excluded masters were away for vacation or other reasons, their chief officers substituted into the master's

. . . .

12   TSB Report, 25.

position, as I had been doing for sixteen years. Some of these chief officers were sailing full-time as masters, yet were either never offered or never accepted the excluded position. In my case, I had been sailing as a master 70 to 75 percent of the time. As a union member, I was entitled to overtime and was making more money per year than the excluded masters, but I worked the full year, as opposed to the eight or nine months put in by an excluded master, to earn that. As unionized employees, chief officers also had certain rights and a degree of protection. Weighing the pros and cons of "going excluded" was a complex subject, much contemplated and discussed.

One factor that influenced my decision was my great dissatisfaction at having to sail under certain masters when I was working as chief officer/first mate. The other event that convinced me to make the move from unionized chief officer to excluded master was a two-hour conversation I had with BC Ferries' new vice president of fleet operations, George Capacci, after the corporation offered me a management position. Capacci convinced me that leaving the union would not be a concern, and that as a member of management I would have influence and the ability to effect changes—the right changes. I told Capacci that I would not be tempering my criticism of corporate decisions, which had occasionally been harsh, and he told me he did not want me to become less critical, that he appreciated my candour. I came away from that meeting believing that I finally had the opportunity I needed. For the first time in years I was feeling excited about the future of BC Ferries.

A princess royal. The *Stena Danica* arrives in British Columbia to begin a new life, first as the *Queen of Surrey* and later as the *Queen of the North*, the flagship of BC Ferries. John Denniston/*The Province* photo

The *Queen of the North* prepares for the Inside Passage to Prince Rupert route, loading passengers and vehicles in Bear Cove, Port Hardy, on a spring day in 2001. Jim Thorne/Wett Coast/Flickr photo

A queen's regalia: four examples of the various colour schemes worn by the *Queen of the North*. R.N. Pearson illustration

Out to pasture: their job done, our lifeboats sit at rest in Patricia Bay. Note the life jackets sitting inside. Lynn Salmon photo

For twenty years she was the biggest ship in the BC Ferries fleet, yet her rescue boat was the smallest. The idea that I might have to launch this boat during a gale in Hecate Strait always made my blood run cold. Here is the rescue boat alongside No. 2 Lifeboat during a routine drill. D. Rutherford photo

The equipment on the navigating bridge—indeed, throughout the ship—represented a range of vintages, from the 1960s right up to 2006. The pale green radars on the port side are the superb CAS 340s. They were replaced before the final voyage. Lynn Salmon photo

Southbound again: the *Queen of the North* is ready to depart Prince Rupert for a trip to Vancouver Island. D. Rutherford photo

Karen Briker, quartermaster. Not long before the last voyage of the *Queen of the North*, I happened to see Karen in a downtown Prince Rupert store, picking out a bicycle for a very excited young boy: her son. Karen's life, like all of ours, was drastically changed by the sinking, but I always remember her as she was that day in Prince Rupert. Photo courtesy Karen Briker

Wright Sound, where the *Queen of the North's* final voyage was ended. Andrew S. Wright/www.cold-coast.com photo

Near the end, a dying ship. Graham Clarke photo

Final resting place: the *Queen of the North* lies below 1,400 feet (427 metres)of water at the bottom of Wright Sound. Photo courtesy Transportation Safety Board

Hundreds of life jackets floated free from the sinking ship. When the first Coast Guard vessel arrived, the life jackets looked to the crew like bodies floating with outstretched arms. The Canadian Coast Guard ship *W.E. Ricker* (on which I was at one time the second mate) is in the background, continuing the search for the two missing passengers. The Canadian Press/Richard Lam photo

The village of Hartley Bay provided refuge for approximately two-thirds of the survivors. The Canadian Press/Richard Lam photo

Two crosses on Gil Island are a memorial for missing passengers Shirley Rosette and Gerald Foisy. Jim Thorne/Wett Coast/Flickr photo

CHAPTER 2

GET UP!

MARCH 21, 2006, WAS A CLEAR, SPRING DAY. WE HAD ARRIVED IN Prince Rupert from Skidegate around five in the afternoon, and we sailed from Prince Rupert at eight o'clock, right on time, bound for Port Hardy on Vancouver Island with two stops along the way. Weather was clear, wind light.

An hour or so before sailing, I had a visitor in my cabin. Edward Dahlgren was a BC Ferries superintendent to whom I reported directly. He and several other managers were travelling on the ship that night. We discussed fuel consumption and other operational matters, and he asked about the photos of my family and toyed with the Leica camera that I had left sitting on my desk.

Like George Capacci, Edward was part of a new team put in place after BC Ferries underwent reorganization as a quasi-private company in 2003, when David Hahn had been appointed president of the company. Edward had ideas for improving the company and, like me, was excited about the future of BC Ferries.

Once we got clear of Prince Rupert harbour, Edward joined me on the bridge. With him was Jason Bowman, the terminal manager at Prince Rupert. Edward was keen on efficiency and had innovative ideas about how we could achieve it. Fuel consumption and scheduling were the topics tonight. I demonstrated the fuel monitor and the various power settings.

Fuel management had been a peeve of mine for many years; I was glad to see someone taking an interest.

I left the bridge a little later than normal, at around 9:00 p.m. PST. There are certain portions of the passage where I make it a rule to be on the bridge. The transit through Tolmie Channel, around Boat Bluff, and through Sarah Passage is one such portion due to its narrowness, blind corners, and acute course changes, which must be perfectly planned and executed. I had about six hours to rest before I would have to be back on the bridge for this section of the voyage. I went to my cabin, took half an hour to "unwind," and turned in.

When I awoke, it was to the sound of the quartermaster, Karen Briker, pounding on my door and frantically shouting, "Get up! Get up! Get up to the bridge! Right now!"

I went to the door and called, "All right, I'm coming," pulled on my pants and started to put on my boots. Before I got my boots on and laced, the ship grounded. I knew what it was straight away. There was no mistaking that sickening sound.

BANG! She struck. BANG! BANG! ... BANG! She struck again and again.

In my mind's eye I could see the ship running along the coast of an island, crashing on the rocks, tree branches sweeping her sides. Years before I had sailed in icebreakers. Same sound, same concussing shocks, and the ship tilting from side to side, objects sliding off the desk and hitting the deck. But this was not icebreaking. This was grounding! I knew we were in serious trouble.

I didn't waste time on a shirt, just grabbed my jacket and raced out and up to the bridge.

The alarm bell was sounding a continuous, deafening ring. The alleyway was full of crew headed out of their cabins, each to their own station. Engineers running aft to the engine room; mates running forward to the bridge.

Second Mate Keven Hilton had already reached the bridge and put the control levers from ahead to full astern, but nothing happened—the propellers had been torn out of the ship.

When I reached the bridge I took one look out the window and one look at the radar. They didn't tell me much. Except for a lone white light a few miles away, there was nothing out the window but black. The radar was set to the half-mile (0.93-kilometre) range, so all I could see was that we were very near a shore.[1] I didn't have time to mess with the radar right then. I grabbed the microphone for the public address (PA) system. (Mercifully, someone had shut off the alarm bells.)

"Attention all passengers and crew," I said. "This is the Captain speaking. All passengers and crew proceed immediately to boat and raft stations on Deck 7. All passengers and crew proceed immediately to boat and raft stations on Deck 7."

At the same time I switched on all the outer deck lights.

When a ship goes aground, just about all the information you need is underwater; you can't see it. So after calling everyone to stations, the next thing to do was to make the ship as secure as possible. This meant closing the two open watertight doors on Deck 1 without delay. This would stop the flow of water from one compartment to another and greatly increase our chances of surviving. A lever in the wheelhouse controlled these doors. All I had to do was throw it from the "open" position to "close." One big problem, though: there were men on duty in the engine room. The doors would close with a crushing power that could kill a man if he was going through the opening at that time. I thought of the engineer who had been crushed to death in exactly that way on board the *Queen of Prince Rupert*. If I closed the doors without first finding out where the engineers were, I ran the risk of crushing someone. I might also be cutting off their escape. There were secondary escape routes in each of the engine room spaces, but without knowing what damage had been done down there, what injuries the personnel might have suffered, or what obstacles might have fallen into their paths, I could not be sure that closing the doors was not sealing their doom.

Three separate telephone systems connected the bridge to the engine room. I tried each one and got no answer. While I was doing that, First Mate Richard St. Pierre was calling on the handheld radio. He got no answer either.

I now had to make the toughest decision of my life. Days later, Edward Dahlgren told me he would never forget the tortured look on my face.

. . . .

1   For those readers who are not marine navigators, the radar would normally be set at a 6- or maybe 12-mile (11- or 22-kilometre) range in these waters, with, possibly, the occasional but momentary view on a larger or smaller scale. To leave it set at a half-mile range is extremely unusual.

"*Close the watertight doors.*"

The First Mate picked up the PA microphone: "Stand clear of watertight doors. All watertight doors are closing *now*. Stand clear of watertight doors. *Stand clear of watertight doors.*"

The control panel for the watertight doors has two pins that stop the lever from being moved accidentally. A hand crank must be turned a number of times to retract the pins. As soon as the crank begins to turn, a warning bell sounds at each watertight door. The crank takes time to retract the pins, so the alarm bells are sounding for several seconds before the doors can close. Once the pins are retracted, the lever is moved to "close," and the watertight doors shut.

My heart was pounding so hard that when I looked down, I could see my chest wall moving in and out with every beat. Experience had taught me to pay no attention to that. Like the alarm bells and all the other sounds of an emergency, my heart was just doing what it's supposed to do.

Third Mate Shiney O'Neill took out an 18-by-24-inch sheet of Plexiglas and laid it on her workstation desk. This was the emergency checklist, modelled on one developed by John McKinnon, a highly efficient first mate I'd once served under, and modified by me for use on the *North*. Despite many recommendations by Transport Canada and numerous requests from me, BC Ferries had never got around to providing the vessel with an evacuation plan, and my checklist was going to have to serve in its place. Shiney would be using a marker to check off each item completed, and she would keep the log. She was also the designated communicator.

I gave the order for flares to be fired. Thinking that the ship was still aground, I ordered the anchors be let go. This was to try to prevent the ship from sliding off the rocks into deep water. Once I learned our position, though, I knew that anchors wouldn't save the ship.

Five decks down, below the waterline, sleeping crew were violently awakened by the noise and shock as the ship hammered onto the rocky shore. Most of the crew jumped out of bed and into water that was over their ankles; some were in it to their knees; some were in it up to their waists.

Marilyn Letendre got a rude awakening and a gash on her head when the semi-submerged mountain named Gil Island came crashing through her cabin wall. Blood streamed down her face as she ran along the hallway through the crew quarters, pounding on doors and calling for everyone to get out.

Lynn Cloutier jumped out of her bed into cold water and found her cabin door barred by a large locker that had broken free and fallen across it. The locker had been bolted to the bulkhead, but the bulkhead had buckled as the force of the grounding was transmitted up through the frames. The locker was very heavy, weighed down with enough gear and uniforms for two crew members for two weeks. Lynn is not a very large woman, and her desperate efforts to move the locker were failing. The incoming water was frigid and getting deeper fast. In the alley outside her cabin, her shipmates pounded on her door and yelled, "Open the door! *For Christ's sake open the door!*"

Lynn put all her strength into it, but the fallen locker wouldn't budge. She was calling out her husband's name and calling out for God. But her husband was at home, and God remained silent. She told me later that she couldn't take the cold and the exertion, so she got back onto her bunk.

She was giving up.

She sat on the bunk and said a prayer to God, asking Him to look after her in death and to look after her family for her.

But God was having none of that.

CRASH! The bulkhead buckled again and more water came rushing into the cabin. In the darkness before her, her grandchildren appeared in a vision. "Gramma, you need to get out of here. We need you."

With the cold ocean water now up to her chest and the vision of her children and grandchildren vivid in her mind, she made a supreme effort. Four feet of water covered the locker. Scrabbling at the side, she somehow got enough of a grip to lift one side, then got her legs under. Not for nothing did she have a lifetime of power-skating behind her. Screaming for God's help and pushing with all her might, she raised the locker clear of the door.

But she wasn't free yet.

The water in the cabin was deeper than it was outside her door, which opened inward. Again she made a huge effort and somehow pulled the door open in spite of the water pressure. She half swam out the door and struggled through the deep water until she was partway up the stairs, then ran the rest of the way—up five decks—to her life raft station.

"By endurance we conquer," said Ernest Shackleton, and how right he was. Courage, adrenalin, faith in God, and a fighting will saved Lynn's life, but she has never recovered from the physical or emotional strain.

⊗

Water was coming in fast. The First Mate, after failing to reach the engineers by radio, headed down the stairs and found that the water was already up to the car deck (Deck 3), about six feet above the load waterline. The Second Mate also headed down, calling out and looking for people, but he too was driven back by the flooding.

"Captain, the water is over the rubbing strake."

A look over the side confirmed that the water was above the rubbing strake, level with the car deck. This meant the ship was going to the bottom. Out in the deep water, there was no power on earth that could save her. All propulsion had been lost, and the ship was listing more and more to starboard.

I got on the PA again and ordered all passengers to proceed immediately to the port side. Then I gave the order to bring boats and rafts to the embarkation level and commence evacuation.

Within seconds of the grounding, the Second Mate had transmitted a distress signal to the Canadian Coast Guard's Marine Communications and Traffic Services (MCTS or "Traffic") in Prince Rupert.[2] Prince Rupert broadcast a Mayday Relay. The Third Mate gave them our position in relation to Sainty Point. Traffic was now asking that the position be expressed in latitude and longitude—a long series of numbers. An error in any of the numbers would mean Traffic had the wrong position. Given the length of this string of digits, the multitude of instruments that were placed far from

· · · · · · · · · · · · ·

2   According to the Marine Communications and Traffic Services website (http://www.ccg-gcc.gc.ca/Marine-Communications/Home), "MCTS centres provide vessel traffic services and waterway management, broadcast weather and safety information; sail plan services in addition to support for other government and marine agencies. The Canadian Coast Guard, Western Region, operates three Vessel Traffic Services Zones: Vancouver, Tofino and Prince Rupert." MCTS "provides marine safety communications co-ordination with the Joint Rescue Co-ordination Centre in Victoria." The system has a radar array on a small portion of the busiest parts of the southern BC Coast, but none on the northern portion.

each other all over the wheelhouse, and the fact that the crew was trying to get the information out as fast as possible, it is not surprising there were errors in the number sent. Traffic also made at least one error in plotting the position. Later, accident investigators made a similar error plotting the latitude and longitude. An accurate geographical position had already been given. I grabbed the microphone and transmitted our position as a range and compass bearing from Point Cumming on Gribbell Island. Traffic persisted in its demand for latitude and longitude. I left it to the Third Mate and got on with the evacuation.

All of this took place in a very few minutes. Third Engineer Roger Tew—in the engine room at the time of the grounding—was now at his station at No. 2 Liferaft Davit (a davit is a type of derrick or crane). He reported that everyone was out of the engine room, and he described the flow of water coming into the engine room from below and from aft. He was so calm and matter-of-fact he could have been describing an everyday occurrence. Someone asked if the bilge pumps were running and he said, "Yes, but it won't make any difference. They'll never keep up. It's like the Slocan River down in that engine room."

With the engine room flooded, the ship's main electrical generators were out of service. The emergency generator, high and dry on Deck 8, kicked in automatically, supplying electrical power to critical systems. When Chief Engineer Brian Erickson was turned back from the engine room by the rushing water, he went straight to the emergency generator to make sure it was running properly and delivering power. He then reported this directly to me.

Two decks below the bridge, Night Steward Eric Lündgren was on duty in the purser's office. Chief Steward Carol Wendschuh and Second Steward Joanne Pierce were there in minutes flat. Every cabin and every passenger area had to be searched, and the passengers directed to the boat and raft stations on Deck 7.

I had designed the original cabin search system after I joined the ship in 1989, and I refined it over the years. Every week we held a fire drill and a boat drill, and I made sure a review of the respective procedures was part of every drill. Cabin searches were included in every fire drill. Tonight, the effectiveness of those drills was going to be put to the test.

According to procedure, each Passenger Control Team member reported in, and the Steward checked off their names, positions, and search areas on a master plan, then gave each team member a flashlight, a master key, and a piece of chalk. The chalk would be used to mark a large X on the cabin doors as each cabin was searched.

The procedure for each individual cabin was to unlock the door, call out, and make a thorough search. This included looking into the washrooms and under the beds. Children, and sometimes even adults, have been known to hide in such emergencies. No assumptions can be made. Included in the search plan were the passenger lounges and the cafeteria. (These were closed at the time of the grounding.)

After Passenger Control Team members finished searching their respective areas, they reported back to the purser's office, where the steward would mark the master plan accordingly. If followed closely, the procedure would ensure that no cabin was missed. But, as I often repeated to my crew during drills, we are only going to do this because something has gone terribly wrong. Don't expect everything else to go perfectly.

On the night of March 22, 2006, more than one thing had gone terribly wrong. Most members of the Passenger Control Team had been in their cabins below the waterline and had to save their own lives first. Right off the bat, the team suffered a critical loss of manpower. Then when the Second Steward reached into a cabinet and drew out the supply box, she discovered that all the chalk was missing, removed by someone during the recent refit.

There was no way around it, no time to correct these problems; the depleted crew would have to do the best they could and proceed to conduct the search shorthanded and without the benefit of chalk to mark the doors. Being shorthanded was more than just a manpower problem, it was an organizational problem, too. The team in the purser's office did their best to compensate. They paid special attention to the cabin manifest (not a true manifest in the strict sense of the term but a spreadsheet) that showed which of the cabins were occupied. In this way, no occupied cabin was left unsearched.

Most of the crew who came from their cabins below had had little time to get dressed. A few were in pyjamas; some had coveralls they had grabbed as they left. Many were barefoot, and some were soaking wet. Up on Deck 7, a number of Mustang anti-exposure suits were available and handed out. A couple of seamen donned firefighter suits, and some took pairs of firefighter gumboots. The Night Steward, whose cabin was on Deck 7, got clothing from his cabin and handed it out. I remember looking at a couple of the women crew who were still in pyjamas and wondering why they weren't dressed. I knew nothing about the drama below. Not one of them complained or cried or made any sound other than what was required to carry out their emergency duties. The clear thinking and self-less courage of those people—seamen, cooks, engineers, mates, stewards, catering attendants—saved our lives. Every one of them was a lifeboatman, working as one crew with one purpose.

They dragged the heavy rafts into place and fastened the lifting hooks. Lynn Cloutier's hands were too numb to connect the hooks, but she operated the slewing gear: seven turns to swing out the davit, then crank the winch handle, lift the fall, inflate the raft. Together the lifeboatmen secured the bowsing lines and conducted passengers and crew into the raft. Ironically, frightened passengers held on to Lynn's hands tightly. Trooper that she is, this traumatized woman reassured them, calmed them, and delivered them to their safety.

Each of the lifeboats was rated to hold fifty-seven passengers. This rating is strictly nominal, based on a formula that takes the volume of the lifeboat and allows ten cubic feet per person. However, the formula does not subtract the space taken up by the engine, the fuel tank, the drinking water tank, the stores locker, etc., so fifty-seven people would be squished in very tightly. I have never seen a lifeboat loaded to capacity. I have often thought about trying it in drills, but the prospect seemed so unsafe I doubted it could be done without injury. We used the lifeboats for some people but relied on rafts for the majority.

A life raft has no means of propulsion, and the site of a sinking ship is a dangerous place. Water will rush into any opening, and anything or anyone nearby can be swept in. Windows blow out as trapped air is pressurized by water from below. Wooden stair treads, railings, gratings, stowage lockers, chairs, etc., break free and come to the surface at high velocity. To escape this danger, the rafts must be towed clear. They can be towed by a motorized lifeboat, but a light rescue boat is more manoeuvrable, so the rescue or shepherd boat, with its two-man crew of Rob Burn and Dave Baker, was the first vessel launched from the ship.

The lifeboats on the *Queen of the North* were stowed suspended from two large hooks, one at each end of the boat, in a kind of cradle above the deck. This is called a "gravity davit" because gravity is the only force used in their launching. Launching procedure is very simple. Several pre-launch checks are made and then two wire ropes, called "gripes," are released, a brake handle is raised, and the boat lowers. The brakeman brings it down to the embarkation deck.

On this night, a gripe swung in when the boat was lowered and perfectly lassoed a cleat on the davit. It was a stunt you couldn't have pulled off in a hundred years if you had tried. With the weight of several tons on it, no man on earth could pull it free. The solution was to either cut it or rig the winch handle and manually haul the heavy boat up until the weight came off the rope. Led by Fourth Mate Karl Lilgert, the crew of No. 2 Lifeboat hauled the boat up.

One raft failed to inflate fully and was cast adrift. Another, loaded with passengers, snagged its inflation lanyard while being lowered. This is why a seaman always carries a knife.

My crew did their job. They did it calmly, efficiently, and safely. There was no shouting, no confusion, no panic.

The passengers were also exemplary. At one point I watched two men who were assisting people into a raft and wondered for a second if we hadn't gained two new crew members I didn't know about, so well did they respond to the emergency.

No. 2 Lifeboat got away successfully, as did the life rafts. The shepherd boat towed the rafts a safe distance from the ship and lashed them together, along with No. 2 Lifeboat. The count of evacuees at this point was eighty-five people. Three people were on the bridge, eleven were in No. 1 Lifeboat (on the starboard side), and two men stood by her to launch. I was alone on the port side of Deck 7.

I looked through the doors to the interior of the ship. On such a dark night the interior looked stark and empty under its bright, artificial lights. The passenger cabins were grouped together at the after ends of Decks 6 and 7. It took me very little time to run through the area, wrenching each cabin door open and looking in. It wasn't a thorough search but a fast last-minute check.

When I got back to Deck 7, the people in No. 1 Lifeboat were hollering for us to get going. On the bridge, Shiney O'Neill worked her station, communicating with Coast Guard, keeping a log, maintaining the checklist. She worked with a peculiar concentration, aware of everything around her but undistracted, as if she were paying attention to the hubbub and ignoring it all at the same time.

I took a quick look over the checklist, noted that Derek Sweet, who was onboard as Familiarizing First Mate (meaning he was learning the tasks of that position), had the log book under his arm, and said, "Let's go."

(It wasn't until we were in the lifeboat that Derek told me he'd had to put the log book down to deal with more urgent matters and it got left behind.)

Shiney didn't move to go but picked up the microphone.

I said, "Shiney, let's go. Time to go."

Still she remained motionless. I don't know if it was her dedication to her duty or if she was so far "in the zone" that she didn't hear me, but she would not move.

Derek had a go. "Shiney, you have to drop that now. It's time to get off the ship."

The men in No. 1 Lifeboat had a clear view of a ship that was half-submerged and sinking deeper by the second. The hollering got louder.

This time I raised my voice. "Shiney! Come on! It's time to go! Let's go!"

Edward Dahlgren is a very skookum lad. Shiney is about five foot two. He picked her up and carried her out the door.

There's an old saying, "One hand for yourself, one hand for the ship." This meant I could carry one thing. I chose a megaphone.

Two tackles held the lifeboat against the ship's side. Oiler Tyrell Derry and Seaman Ryan Johnson stood by them, ready to launch. Edward, Derek, and Shiney boarded the lifeboat.

I gave the order, "Ease the bowsing-in tackles." The tackles were eased, the boat moved away from the ship's side, the tackles were unshipped.

One often finds there is a difference between what he has been taught and what people actually practise. This might have been what prompted Ryan to ask one of the engineers if he should slide the now out-of-use tackle into the lifeboat. Since it would normally be used only when the boat returned to the ship, he received a sarcastic answer from one of the lifeboat crew.

"Do it the way you were trained," I told him.

He slid the tackle down its own fall, just the way the book says.

"Lower away" was my next order.

The boat dropped to the water with a splash. Immediately, the crew released the hooks, released the painter (bow line), and fired up the engine. I motioned to Tyrell and Ryan to head down the Jacob's ladder (a rope ladder).

I came down last.

There are big letters on the side of the ship that say BC *Ferries*. These letters are about ten feet tall. As I passed them, I saw they were half covered in water. Technically, the ship was already sunk, kept afloat only by the "unofficial" buoyancy of the car deck superstructure.

When we joined the shepherd boat, No. 2 Lifeboat, and the rafts a safe distance from the sinking ship, it was time to take stock of the condition of the people. There were a few injuries to the crew, cuts mostly. No one was bleeding profusely anymore, but they did need attention. The worst injury was to Marilyn Letendre. She had escaped with her life but carried a good-sized gash behind her ear. Oiler John Panlilio had escaped the engine room but he paid a price; his hand seemed to be broken. He, like all the others, made no complaint.

I sent the shepherd boat, with my Second Mate in charge, back toward the ship to look out for any people in the water or on board.

Two nearby fishing boats—the *April Augusta* and the *Lone Star*—arrived on scene while we were still abandoning ship. Using searchlights, they also circled the ship and reported seeing no one.

Bringing the megaphone turned out to be a good decision; I could speak quietly and still command attention.

"Is anyone missing a travelling companion?" I asked. No answer.

Head count was next. Although we were all together, this proved to be difficult. Each boat and raft had to conduct its own count, with flashlights the only available lighting. (There was an Aldis lamp, but it would have been blinding.) We had to keep stopping, going back, and recounting. With so many recounts, I was never really satisfied with the number. BC Ferries was also not sure how many people they had put on the ship. At one point they decided it must be ninety-nine and announced that all aboard had been saved.[3] They had to retract this later when it was discovered the correct number was 101. The system then in place for tracking both passengers and crew was flawed, in my opinion, and it was one of the safety issues for which I had suggested improvements in the past. Nevertheless, I was well aware at the time that the count was in doubt, and communicated this clearly to the Coast Guard, who proceeded to carry out an intensive search.

· · · · · · · · · · · · ·

3   Steve Mertl and Terri Theodore, "Residents Hailed as Heroes for Saving Passengers after B.C. Ferry Sinks; All the 100 or so Passengers Rescued," Saint John (NB) *Telegraph-Journal*, March 23, 2006. The next day, one of these journalists wrote a new story: Steve Mertl, "Two Passengers Believed Dead in B.C. Ferry Sinking; Questions Raised about Safety of Queen of the North," Saint John (NB) *Telegraph-Journal*, March 24, 2006.

We watched the dying ship. One part of me wished for some miracle to save her; the other just wished that if she was going to sink, could she please hurry up. Edward stood beside me and put his hand on my arm, knowing that I was losing a loved one. All I could think was "my beautiful ship."

I had pulled my windbreaker on as I ran to the bridge. Once the evacuation started, I took my coat from the hook and put it on over top. Over that I wore the regulation life jacket. There is a whistle permanently attached to my coat, and I keep the pockets loaded. Reaching into them, I could feel my flashlight, a knife, a small adjustable wrench, a small pair of needle-nose Vise-Grips, a multi-tip screwdriver, 100 feet (30 metres) of parachute cord, matches, my handheld radio with spare battery—things I might need on a night like this. There was also a set of keys with a short lanyard. The lanyard was a souvenir of one of my daughter's trips. I took it out and showed it to Edward. The writing on the lanyard read I'D RATHER BE FLYING.

My beautiful ship was sinking lower and lower. The list had stabilized at around 9 degrees. The bow was slightly raised.

When the starboard rail was just about touching the surface of the sea, the bow rose. That's when the rumbling sounds began. It must have been the noise of the cars sliding to the stern.

The bow rose steadily. Now the rumbling noise was joined by the sight of water spraying through the windows as they shattered under the pressure. Some of what we saw might have been dust, freed from where it had collected in the false deckheads. Many people mistook it for steam.

The bow kept on rising until it was absolutely vertical. About a third of the ship's length was showing. Waterfalls ran out of the holes in her hull from her bow right down the full length to where her new waterline was.

And then she sank.

Straight down, straight as an arrow, she disappeared. She was gone.

CHAPTER 3

SURVIVAL

THE RESPONSIBILITIES OF A SHIP'S MASTER DO NOT END WHEN HIS ship sinks. The safety and survival of the passengers and crew remain uppermost in his mind. Injuries need to be assessed and attended to, as do medical conditions. I remembered that one passenger was diabetic and would be needing medication before too long. Another reported high blood pressure and would also need medication.

Cold was an immediate concern, especially for those who were wet. Rain had started falling, so soon everyone was going to be wet. The two lifeboats and the shepherd boat were open to the weather, and those aboard had only the clothes they were wearing to protect them from the rain.

The occupants of the rafts were somewhat better off, having the protection of a canopy that practically made the raft into a tent. The floor of a life raft is a double-bottom chamber that inflates to provide insulation from the cold sea water, but don't get the idea that a life raft is a comfortable place to be. It isn't. We had already seen one life raft fail to inflate fully during the evacuation (it was discarded). If the double-bottom floors of any of the other rafts failed to inflate, it would not be the first time in maritime history it went undetected.

HARTLEY BAY

The Hartley Bay Indian Reserve is 6 miles (11 kilometres) from where the *Queen of the North* sank. The marine VHF radio is as commonplace there as the telephone is in most other communities, so the Mayday call rang through kitchens and living rooms on the reserve. The people of Hartley Bay knew what to do: they got in their boats and came out. Those who stayed behind prepared hot food and drink and got the community hall ready to receive survivors.

When boats arrived from the village of Hartley Bay, I decided to take advantage of their presence. I would send those who were injured, needing medical attention, or less able to cope with the conditions because of age or infirmity back to the village so they could be taken care of. I would also have given priority to those who were wet, but every crew member—even those who were soaked—remained silent. I was unaware of what they endured until long after it was over.

Putting my Chief Steward in charge, I sent sixty-four passengers and crew into Hartley Bay, seventeen of them with the *Lone Star* and the rest with the local boats.

Looking back, that is one thing I might have done differently. If I had waited a little longer, all the survivors would have gone aboard the Coast Guard ship *Sir Wilfrid Laurier*, which arrived shortly after and also took excellent care of everyone. The *Laurier* could have taken them directly to Prince Rupert, eliminating two inconvenient transfers. Although the cold and wet were factors, our situation in the boats and rafts was far from urgent. The people of Hartley Bay were wonderful and deserved to be praised for the hospitality and assistance they extended throughout the affair. But splitting our group between two locations created logistical problems and delayed an accurate head count.

Two people—Gerald Foisy and Shirley Rosette—disappeared that night. We may never know what happened to them.

CHANGING COUNTS

The *Queen of the North* struck the ground at 0021:20 PST on March 22, 2006.[1] There is no record of the exact time the last person left the ship,

. . . .

1   This time is from the TSB Report, page 6, which took it from the ship's electronic chart system computer, retrieved by submersible between June 15 and 17, 2006, so it should be accurate. All other times in this chronology are taken from the Incident Log at the Joint Rescue Co-ordination Centre (please see Appendix E).

but at 0056 PST, the Joint Rescue Co-ordination Centre (JRCC) in Victoria received the report from MCTS that we had abandoned ship. There would have been some delay in that message getting to them, so the best we can say is that the abandonment was completed before 0056 PST.

It was a little after 0130 when we watched the *Queen of the North* sink. (At 0139, JRCC made a log book entry noting it had received the report of sinking, relayed from the *Lone Star*.)

A Fast Response Craft (FRC), sent ahead by the *Sir Wilfrid Laurier*, arrived on the scene at 0159. It found the surface of the sea strewn with hundreds of life jackets that had floated free, and large pieces of teak that had broken loose and shot to the surface. In the sparse lighting available to the crew, these objects appeared as bodies lying flat in the water with arms out to the sides. In fact, it was the tapes of the life jackets that were lying outstretched. Navigating through the debris field, the FRC couldn't travel at full speed for fear it might run over a survivor or a body.

From this point, the plan shifted to transferring the remainder of the survivors onto the Coast Guard ship *Sir Wilfrid Laurier*, which arrived at 0210. Some were taken by the FRC; the rest remained in the lifeboats, and we motored over to the ship together.

The *Laurier* lowered its accommodation ladder—a kind of portable staircase that lies alongside the ship—and our lifeboat nosed up to it. Everyone came up the ladder, and then the *Laurier*'s crew hoisted our boats on board with their derrick.

Thirty-three of us gathered inside the ship's accommodation. Karl Lilgert, the fourth mate, who had been navigating when the *Queen of the North* went aground, looked like death, pale and ill.

I had turned to talk to someone when Tyrell Derry tapped me on the shoulder and said, "Cap, Karl just went outside. Should I go with him?"

"Yes, stay with him," I said. From that point on I was more concerned about Karl's mental well-being than just about anything else. Would he be suicidal? I didn't know, but I was not going to take any chances.

The *Laurier*'s crew got us organized. They put Karl in a separate room with a couple of Coast Guard people and one of the *Queen of the North*'s mates to look after him. He sat on the deck with his knees drawn up and his face hidden between them. The ship's Rescue Specialist, a paramedic, kept an eye on him.

The rest of the crew settled into the mess and the *Laurier* crew's TV room. I spent most of my time on the bridge, going down every so often to see how my crew was doing.

Right from the time of the abandonment, vessels had carried on a search for possible survivors in the water. When the *Laurier* arrived, she took on the role of On-Scene Co-ordinator (OSC), taking direction from the JRCC and organizing the actions of all the resources on the scene.

The biggest difference between conducting a search on the ground and conducting a search on the water is that people and things on the water will always be moved by the wind and current. You will have little success if you search at the site of a sinking. Everyone and everything is floating away pretty much the entire time. One of the first things the *Laurier* did was to drop a data-marking buoy, a free-floating buoy designed to duplicate the set and drift (that is, the direction and speed caused by current) of a person in the water.[2] Positional information obtained from the buoy is used to plan the search. By this method, the search area is moved in step with the set and drift.

Wright Sound is the junction of seven channels: Princess Royal (McKay Reach), Whale, Lewis, Cridge, Grenville, Douglas, and Verney. The OSC immediately deployed search vessels, both government and civilian craft, to set up barriers at the entrance to each channel, cutting off the escape of anything or anyone being carried by the wind and current. With those barriers established, the remaining craft carried out geometrical search patterns and shoreline searches in accordance with the instructions from JRCC. At least sixteen vessels and three aircraft covered the search area, which was kept lit by parachute illumination flares dropped from the Buffalo search aircraft. Shore crews searched the beaches as well as the interior of Gil Island.[3]

As the search went on, we also needed to pay attention to those who were in Hartley Bay or on board the *Laurier*. Some lacked clothing; others needed first aid. Working together, we drew up plans for dealing with the injured. The Coast Guard started lining up critical incident stress debriefers for when we arrived in Prince Rupert.

. . . .

2   Strictly speaking, "set" refers to movement caused by current. "Drift" (or leeway) refers to movement caused by wind. With a person in the water, drift is negligible, but the colloquial phrase "set and drift" is used universally.

3   BC Ministry of Public Safety and Solicitor General, "Coroner's Report into the Death of Gerald Victor Joseph Foisy," Case No. 2006-0701-0010, September 16, 2010, accessed on BC Coastal Transportation Society website, July 6, 2016, http://bccoastaltransportation .ca/wp-content/uploads/2016/03/Foisy-G-CR.pdf

In Hartley Bay, the people off the *Queen of the North* gathered in the community hall. Local residents supplied them with hot drinks and food. The Chief Steward tallied up the numbers and did her best to keep them together. Frequently, people left the hall to have a cigarette, grab a breath of air, or make a cell phone call.

There was a telephone at the community hall, but it could not accept incoming calls. The *Laurier* had a satellite phone, so when I needed to talk to someone in Hartley Bay, I had to call on the *Laurier*'s radio and get the Chief Steward to phone the ship.

At 0305, Hartley Bay reported that they had a count of passengers and crew totalling sixty-eight.

At 0327, Hartley Bay reported a total of sixty-four survivors. There were thirty-eight of us on the *Laurier*, for a grand total of 102.

At 0338, Hartley Bay confirmed a total of sixty-four survivors.

At 0343, a recount on board confirmed thirty-seven survivors aboard the *Laurier*. The total accounted for was now 101.

At 0352, a recount in Hartley Bay confirmed sixty-five survivors. Total was now 102.

At 0536, a recount in Hartley Bay confirmed sixty-three survivors. Total was now one hundred.

During the abandonment, Edward Dahlgren had grabbed the satellite phone and torn the phone directory off the bulkhead of the *North*. Before we were off the ship, he phoned BC Ferries vice president George Capacci and told him the unbelievable news. Staff members in Victoria and Prince Rupert rushed to their respective offices and were kept busy. One of the tasks for our personnel department in Prince Rupert was to telephone the families of the crew and let them know what had happened and that we were safe. When I had a minute to spare, I gave my wife a quick phone call. Otherwise, I was busy monitoring the progress of the search, assessing and planning for the needs of the survivors, and drinking endless cups of tea on the bridge of the *Laurier*.

With Edward Dahlgren and Jason Bowman, the two BC Ferries managers from Prince Rupert who had been aboard the *North*, I tried to anticipate all the needs in addition to the first aid requirements. Most people would have left their wallets behind and would have no money, no identification, and no possessions other than what they happened to have in their pockets. They were going to need accommodation, cash, clothing, a car insurance representative, transportation … all manner of everyday things.

Our concern about the mental states of Karl Lilgert and Karen Briker, who had been the quartermaster at the wheel when the ship ran aground, was pressing. The *Laurier*'s captain, first mate, and I discussed the need to get them and the injured to hospital. Two Royal Canadian Air Force rescue helicopters from 442 Squadron in Comox were on scene; one would continue searching while the other prepared to fly people out from the heli-pad in Hartley Bay. The problem was how to transfer those who were still on the *Laurier* to shore. Someone suggested they could be hoisted off by the helicopter, a routine rescue procedure, but the *Laurier*'s first mate, Steve Kennedy, was adamant that Lilgert was in no condition for such a traumatic undertaking. The transfer would have to be done by boat. I selected my First and Second Mates to go with them and make sure they were all looked after. The *Laurier*'s boat carried them to Hartley Bay, where they and the five injured passengers and crew already ashore boarded the Cormorant helicopter, Rescue 907, and flew to Prince Rupert.

The sun rose. I looked out over the sea. My beautiful ship was gone. The British Columbia coast was still and silent. To the north of where we sat, the deep-sea trawler and fisheries research vessel *W.E. Ricker* was on station, continuing the search. Long ago I had been the second mate in that ship. The *Laurier* would soon be sailing, and the *Ricker* would take over as OSC.

At 0728, a recount aboard the *Sir Wilfrid Laurier* came to thirty-six. Total was now ninety-nine: two missing.

The searchers expanded the search area. They went beyond the channel barriers that had been set up and searched as much as 5 nautical miles (9.3 kilometres) farther up every channel. Then they expanded the search area again to take in all of Lewis and Cridge Passages, go completely around Hawkesbury Island, and extend down Douglas Channel.

The *Laurier* sailed into Hartley Bay and stood off. Someone handed me a standard keyhole life jacket, and I went down the *Laurier*'s accommodation ladder to board a Department of Fisheries boat that was waiting there. I disembarked at the Hartley Bay Public Wharf and walked up the ramp to meet Trafford Taylor, executive vice president at BC Ferries, who told me we would be travelling to Prince Rupert by helicopter. I protested that my place was with my crew, but Taylor overruled this objection.

The Coast Guard helicopter was small. We each had a headset with a microphone so we could talk to each other. After takeoff, the pilot asked me if it would be all right to fly over the accident site. I said it was all right with me. We could see exactly where the ship was because the light diesel fuel had formed a delta shape in the current. The apex of the delta was where the ship would be. I suggested he note the position on his GPS.

The helicopter flight to Prince Rupert Coast Guard base in Seal Cove took less than an hour. We landed and I was ushered into the hangar to wait for a ride. There was a telephone in the hangar, so I phoned my parents and assured them I was all right.

That first day in Prince Rupert, a BC Ferries lawyer interviewed me about the accident. Most of the day I sat in my hotel room. I called my brothers and my cousin, and spoke to my family at home again.

The town was completely overrun by the news media. Cameras, tripods, microphones, lights, lighting umbrellas were everywhere. Every hotel room in the city was full.

Just before five o'clock, I watched the arrival of the *Sir Wilfrid Laurier* from my room. The dock was in front of the hotel. A camera crew was set up on a lower balcony, filming the event, unaware that the person they wanted to talk to was right behind them.

Later that evening I got a message that the crew, gathered in a conference room of the hotel, was asking for me. Some of the crew's family members were there as well, along with the BC premier, some company officials, terminal staff, and a long-time friend of the crew, Reverend Peter Hamel, the Anglican priest from Masset. There were also a few off-duty crew who had not made that last trip. They were told they couldn't come in, but their response was "That's our crew. So we'll be going in there."

A ship's crew isn't *like* a family: it *is* a family. Not perfect. Not always who or what we want it to be. We don't always get along as we should, and sometimes we don't even love each other as much as we should. But we stand together.

I have seldom been in a room so full of emotion. It was here that I first heard the stories of what went on down below when the ship grounded. Lynn Cloutier hugged me and her story poured out of her. Marilyn Letendre did the same. I went around the room and saw every crew member, heard their stories, and told them how grateful I was for their courage, their clear-thinking, and their actions. I told them that, more than any-thing, I was grateful they were alive.

On March 23, 2006, the day after the sinking, David Hahn issued a press release. This, in part, is what he said:

> I want to extend my highest commendation to the Queen of the North crew for their response in the face of a tremendously challenging situation when the vessel grounded and was lost in Wright Sound early Wednesday morning.
>
> I am grateful to all employees involved for their response in the face of adversity. The skills and expertise displayed during the evacuation of the vessel was admirable.
>
> ... every one of the passengers who disembarked the coast guard vessel Sir Wilfrid Laurier in Prince Rupert yesterday afternoon had nothing but praise for your actions.
>
> ... I take great pride in the exemplary teamwork that was demonstrated during this extraordinary incident.

The same day, Gordon Campbell, premier of British Columbia, sent a letter to me and to the crew, commending us for our "amazing rescue work on that fateful night," our "professionalism and expertise," and our "selfless courage, co-ordination, co-operation, and heroism." He followed this with a personal letter to me.

I spent four days in Prince Rupert. Rev. Peter Hamel joined me for breakfast in the morning before going out and buying me a watch, something to read, and a large can of coffee. A close friend in town bought me some T-shirts so that I would have something to wear. I had interviews with investigators from the Transportation Safety Board and with BC Ferries lawyers.

Except for those occasions, I left my hotel room only twice. After the media frenzy had wound down a bit, I felt it was safe to go out for a walk. Edward Dahlgren saw me and had me up to his apartment for tea. And one night I ventured to Rodhos Greek Restaurant for dinner. A number of BC Ferries' management and legal team were there, and they kindly invited me to join them.

On the fifth morning, I took a taxi to the airport ferry. The Prince

Rupert airport is across the harbour on Digby Island. To avoid the press, I took the early ferry, which carried the airport staff. As a regular traveller in and out of Prince Rupert for over twenty years, I was known to the airline staff, many of whom had been there since the days of Canadian Pacific Airlines. They gave me a lift from the ferry landing up to the airport terminal, checked me in, and let me hang out in their back room until flight time.

In Vancouver, my brother, sister-in-law, niece, and nephew met me at the airport, along with my boyhood friend and former shipmate Lynn Harrison and his wife, Cathy Lightfoot. There was time for lunch, a good visit, and a much-needed decompression. Then I was on my way home to Calgary.

Anticipation is the greater part of joy. The flight went quickly. The Rocky Mountains shone like gold.

When I stepped off the plane in Calgary, my strides were long and fast. As I neared the top of the down escalator, I could see my family waiting beside the statue of Sam Livingstone, a western pioneer and a friend of my great-grandfather. Home at last.

CHAPTER 4

MAKE NO STATEMENTS

BITTER EXPERIENCE HAS TAUGHT MARINERS OF THE WORLD ABOUT
the dangers of legal proceedings. Professional mariners belong to associations that offer the benefit of legal defence insurance. In Canada, that
association is the Canadian Merchant Service Guild, and the back of every
Guild membership card has the following notice prominently inscribed:

LEGAL DEFENCE INSURANCE

Your involvement in a marine occurrence may result in
your being interviewed by different authorities including the Transportation Safety Board, federal and local
police forces, the Coast Guard and similar authorities
of the United States if the occurrence takes place in
American waters.

MAKE NO STATEMENTS, written or verbal, and SIGN
NO DOCUMENTS until you have consulted the GUILD or
its legal representative.

You are insured, subject to policy conditions, as long
as you remain a member in good standing in accordance
with the National Bylaws. All incidents must be reported
as soon as possible (within 24 or 48 hours).

The administrators of the defence plan, and the Guild executives,
constantly warn members about the dangers of failing to heed legal

advice and acting without representation. Randy O'Neill, senior vice president with Lancer Insurance Company and manager of its Marine License Insurance division since 1984, cites a collision case in which investigators very quickly concluded that one party was completely to blame and immediately suspended the master's licence. Why? Because "in an attempt to explain what happened to Coast Guard investigators, [the master] waived his right to engage counsel and gave a lengthy and rambling verbal description of his account of what had happened, and interspersed his monologue with several mea culpas for being a party to the collision. Consequently, the Coast Guard investigators interpreted his contrition as an admission of fault ... By the time his license defense attorney was finally contacted, assigned, arrived on the scene and interviewed him, the towboat's master had talked himself and his company into a pretty tight spot." The master's company was sued for three million dollars.[1] Note that the advice to make no statements is not just for the benefit of the individual but for his company as well. As a professional, I was well aware of this and had the company's, as well as my own, protection in mind.

I telephoned the Canadian Merchant Service Guild soon after I arrived at my hotel in Prince Rupert on the day of the sinking. The Guild had already sent its lawyer, Jack Buchan, to Prince Rupert. Coincidentally, Jack also represented the British Columbia Ferry and Marine Workers' Union (the Ferry Workers' Union), which I had left just one month earlier when I became an excluded master.

Jack strongly advised me not to talk to the media, so I soon had to get call display on my home telephone. It seemed as if it never stopped ringing. *The Globe and Mail*, the *Vancouver Sun*, the *Province*, the *Victoria Times Colonist*, the *Calgary Herald*, CBC, and the rest of the news media all wanted to interview me. I felt rude not answering the phone, but I could understand the value of Jack's advice.

Before I even got ashore after the sinking, I was making plans for my return to work. I felt perfectly all right, but I knew enough about post-traumatic stress disorder to understand that my return should be made tentatively. I planned on getting some rest and then getting "back in the

· · · · · · · · · · · ·

1   Randy O'Neill, "Loose Lips Sink Ships and Careers," *Marine News*, November 2011, http://www.marinelink.com/news/shipsand-careers-loose341875.aspx

saddle" without much delay. I figured I would probably need to take a month before I could go back to work.

When the month was up, I called Edward Dahlgren, who told me that BC Ferries' decision was that the master and the members of the bridge team would remain on leave until the federal Transportation Safety Board had completed its investigation.

People wonder why investigations take so long. Being involved in the TSB process gave me an insight. Obviously, the investigators need to see whatever physical, electronic, and written evidence there is. They also need to interview the people involved, witnesses, and, sometimes, subject matter experts. Often, an interview will raise a new point. When that happens, the investigators may have to go back to see previous interviewees. When TSB investigators think they've got it right, they print a draft report. Interested persons are issued copies of this report and given the opportunity to respond. The responses are collated and a new draft report is printed. This process is repeated as many times as the TSB investigators feel is necessary until they are satisfied that they've got it right. Then they issue the final report. Getting the report out in under two years is actually pretty impressive. The TSB released its report in March 2008, two years after the sinking, while the report of BC Ferries' Divisional Inquiry, described below, was released in March 2007.

So I waited.

BC FERRIES DIVISIONAL INQUIRY

In April 2006, BC Ferries declared that it would hold its own Divisional Inquiry or DI.[2] It is hard to believe this would have been popular with its lawyers. Anyone who has watched crime shows on TV knows that "anything you say can be held against you." *Anything* you say, that is—not just

. . . .

2   The word "Divisional" does not really have a meaning here. The term originated years ago when BC Ferries had two divisions: Northern and Southern. When there was a major incident, it would be investigated by the other division, so that an accident in the Northern Division would be investigated by management from the Southern Division and vice versa. The terminology was left unchanged despite a reorganization that rendered the procedure obsolete.

what you say to the police. Therefore, anything said or written in the course of a company inquiry can become ammunition for prosecutors and plaintiffs in civil and criminal trials. At this early stage it was unclear what legal fallout there would be from the sinking, but already there was a criminal investigation underway, and at least three lawsuits in the offing. By holding a DI, the corporation was exposing itself and its employees.

Karl Lilgert and Keven Hilton petitioned BC Ferries to make their testimony before the DI privileged and confidential. They had already fully cooperated with the BC Ferries lawyers for the insurance claim, where they had been protected from having their testimony used against them. However, BC Ferries refused to offer the same protection at the DI.[3] Consequently, Lilgert and Hilton showed up at the DI but, on the advice of their respective lawyers, refused to testify on matters that could have put them in jeopardy in the civil suits or exposed them to criminal charges, and refused to talk about the critical period leading up to the grounding. BC Ferries suspended and later fired the two men, along with Karen Briker (who did testify at the DI). This would have implications for me when I appeared before the DI represented by Jack Buchan, the same lawyer who was counselling Karl Lilgert.

I was interrogated for the DI twice, on April 21, 2006, and May 25, 2006.[4]

The members of the board of the Divisional Inquiry into the sinking of the *Queen of the North* were Trafford Taylor (chairman), George Capacci, Blaine Ellis, Mark Collins, and Captain Tom McNeilage.[5] My first interrogation was conducted mainly by Trafford Taylor, who at the time of the sinking

· · · · · · · · · · · ·

3   "Crew's Silence Hurt Ferry Safety," *Victoria Times Colonist*, November 7, 2008. Lilgert and Hilton had also participated in the Transportation Safety Board investigation, but witness statements to the TSB are confidential.

4   Because the proceedings of the Divisional Inquiry were confidential, much of the information on my DI interviews is drawn from the decision of the Workers' Compensation Appeal Tribunal, WCAT-2010-00733 (hereafter WCAT Decision), available online at http://www.wcat.bc.ca/research/decisions/pdf/2010/03/2010-00733.pdf

5   From BC Ferries Divisional Inquiry, "*Queen of the North* Grounding and Sinking," DI #815-06-01 (Victoria: BC Ferries, 2007), 1 and 2, http://www.bcferries.com/about /qnorthdivisionalinquiry.html (hereafter Divisional Inquiry); and British Columbia Ferry Services Inc. and BC Ferry Authority, *Annual Report 2006/07* (Victoria: Author, 2007), 79.

was executive vice president, operations. (Shortly afterward, he became executive vice president, new vessel construction and industry affairs.)

I didn't know it at the time, but the DI had gotten off to a rocky start. It was supposed to have been chaired by the company's director of safety, health and environment, Captain Darin Bowland, and he was flown up to Prince Rupert to begin proceedings. In a Supreme Court affidavit on September 17, 2006, he submitted that he was taken aside by two BC Ferries lawyers who suggested "that the cause of the sinking was crew negligence." When he "pointed out that it was necessary to recognize that BC Ferries had serious systemic safety problems" that may have contributed to the accident, the lawyers "suggested that the way for me to conduct the Inquiry was to not focus on what BC Ferries had done wrong but rather on 'opportunities' for BC Ferries to improve." Later "they suggested that a better way of conducting the Inquiry might be for the lawyers hired by BC Ferries to conduct the interviews and then to pass the information obtained on to the Divisional Inquiry board." Bowland said he then asked the lawyers "if they were suggesting that we should suspend the Inquiry." He took their silence to mean "that it had been decided that I should end the Inquiry" and phoned head office, requesting clarification of the Inquiry status from the company president, David Hahn. After failing to get his concerns satisfied, he went back to Victoria and resigned, not just as chair of the DI, but from his position as director of safety, health and environment, saying "I did not want my ethical standards to be compromised."[6] The DI then resumed with Taylor as chair.

The DI interrogations were not recorded, which, as my lawyer later argued, appeared to violate BC Ferries' Fleet Regulations. Taylor replied "that he had the authority to promulgate Fleet Regulations and therefore could authorize any deviation from them."[7] The only record of the proceedings are handwritten notes taken by members of the DI panel. The notes are not complete and are not verbatim—there are numerous misquotes—and the accuracy and completeness vary from one writer to another. Note-takers added in their own exclamation marks, apparently to

. . . .

6   Bowland's comments are all from Affidavit #1 of Darin Bowland, sworn September 17, 2006, in the Supreme Court of British Columbia, No. S-063817 (Vancouver Registry), http://www.cbc.ca/bc/news/061019_affidavit.pdf

7   WCAT Decision, 63.

add emphasis to items they thought to be important; they do not indicate that the speaker has made an exclamation. Much is left out, there are many gaps, and all of this is obvious to anyone who reads them.[8]

When I arrived for the DI on April 21, the panel seemed to be confused by my choice of lawyer. As I mentioned, Jack Buchan, who was representing me on behalf of the Canadian Merchant Service Guild, had also been retained by the Ferry Workers' Union to represent Karl Lilgert and some of the crew. As the Workers' Compensation Appeal Tribunal (WCAT) later wrote in its decision:

> [107] Before [Captain Henthorne's] first interview with the DI on April 21, 2006 the DI panel had already interviewed three members of the ship's bridge crew, including the 4/O [Fourth Officer Karl Lilgert] and the QM1 [Quartermaster Karen Briker]. They were bargaining unit members and had been accompanied by J [Jack Buchan] who acted as legal counsel for their trade union.[9] During their interviews, they refused to give any evidence about the critical 14-minute period when the ship sailed straight into Gil Island without making a course change. It is undisputed that their refusal to testify in that regard frustrated the purpose of the DI. Under section 9.09 of the Fleet Regulations, the whole purpose of the DI was to produce a report which contained a determination of the cause or contributing factors of the ship incident and to make recommendations for corrective action to prevent a reoccurrence. The DI panel members were frustrated by these witnesses' refusal to testify on key issues at the inquiry proceedings.
>
> [108] The worker [that would be me] appeared at his first DI interview with the same legal counsel, J, who had earlier represented the witnesses who refused to testify at the DI proceedings about key events before the ship grounded. Captain C[apacci] was blunt in his testimony

. . . .

8   WCAT Decision, 34–35, 37, 41, 46, 50, 57–58, 69.

9   In fact, Karen Briker was represented from the start by Chris Giaschi.

that he was insulted when he saw the worker walk in with a "union lawyer."[10] Captain C testified:

> "... it was representative of [the worker's] failure to accept his management responsibility—[the worker] was management and he didn't in my mind need representatives—I was his representative—I was looking out for his best interests and to make sure that we got to the facts ... I expected him to fully participate in the DI to find out what happened."

[109] There was a lot of evidence ... about whether or not at the time of the first DI interview the DI panel members understood that when J appeared with the worker, J was in fact acting on behalf of the Guild rather than the trade union certified as agent for the bargaining unit members. The handwritten notes of the DI panel members are either non-existent or very sketchy on what happened at the outset of the April 21, 2006 interview with the worker. The most thorough notes about the worker's first DI interview are from Captain M[cNeilage] who was then the certified trade union's observer/member on the DI panel.

[110] From Captain M's notes and the oral hearing testimony of Captains C and T[aylor] we find that there was some confusion at the beginning of the interview about why J was there and whether or not the worker, like some of the previous witnesses represented by J, was going to refuse to testify on key issues. From the notes about Captain T's remarks at the worker's interview, we find that Captain T was irritated that J's presence might

• • • • • • • • • • • •

10 Jack Buchan was not a "union lawyer." He was retained by the Ferry Workers' Union and by the Canadian Merchant Service Guild to represent individuals dealing with the marine casualty investigations resulting from the accident.

be a signal that the worker, another key witness, was also
going to refuse to testify on important matters. We do
not find it important to decide whether or not Captain
C clearly understood at the time that J was acting on
behalf of the Guild rather than the certified trade union.
We note that almost two years later the employer's submission to the Board case officer still referred to J as the
"Union's legal representative" so this indicates that the
employer continued to attribute to J the persona of "the
union lawyer" whatever his actual role in acting on the
worker's behalf.[11]

When members of the DI panel saw Jack accompanying me, they apparently sprang to the conclusion that I did not understand my position
as a non-union manager and was somehow allying myself with the union.
They failed to understand that my lawyer's presence was also in the company's interest. They seemed to have forgotten the numerous times that
other masters brought lawyers along to various inquiries over the years.
None of those masters suffered any consequences.

Shortly after the interrogation began, following up on his first question,
Taylor asked me "if there was anything that affected the safety of the ship
that [I] had ever requested to be fixed."[12] I had already told him that I
had raised a number of concerns. When he asked for details, I hesitated,
thinking of the legal considerations and pointing this out to the panel.
Taylor "responded that he did not want to hide anything but in the interests of safety it was important to 'get it out.'"[13] So I described several
concerns, including the absence of more than one evacuation route from
the car deck and the lack of safe guard rails. None of these were directly
related to the sinking, but Taylor continued to press me for information. I
brought up the lack of a passenger count, which had caused problems during the evacuation, and mentioned another issue with rescue boat davits.
It was quite some time before Taylor finally conceded that it was going to
take too long for me to recount every concern that I had. At this point—

. . . .

11 WCAT Decision, 34–35.

12 This section of my DI interview is covered in WCAT Decision, 39–41.

13 WCAT Decision, 39.

probably a good ninety minutes into the interrogation—he asked me to write up a list after I got home and send it to the inquiry panel.[14]

Taylor then asked me why I had taken the job as excluded master with BC Ferries when I had all those concerns. I told him that I had met with George Capacci for two hours before being convinced that I could be part of the solution to the problems if I accepted the position.[15]

Near the end of the interview, Taylor asked if I had any idea about what happened to cause the grounding of the ship. I said I had an idea, but it was just speculation. When Taylor asked what my idea was, I checked with my lawyer, who said I "could answer as long as it was understood it was just conjecture." I said that since an extension of the *Queen of the North*'s course leading up to Sainty Point would take it to the point of impact on Gil Island, it could be that the ship did not change course. This suggested to me there might have been a problem with the controls on the new autopilot that had been installed when the ship was in for refit.[16]

After the interview I went home and drew up a list of safety concerns, as the panel had requested. The result was "11 typewritten single-spaced pages, describing 58 safety issues" that I had brought up with BC Ferries while I was still a member of the union.[17]

When I appeared before the DI panel the second time, in Nanaimo on May 25, 2006, they acknowledged receipt of my list and asked if any of the concerns on it had caused the grounding. I replied that I did not think any of them were causes and repeated my speculation that it was an issue with the autopilot: "the bridge crew did not get the course set right and when they realized it they had trouble getting the control back."[18] The WCAT noted that Captain Capacci "described the atmosphere at [my] DI interviews as 'frosty.'" I too felt this frostiness and, at the second interview, downright hostility.[19]

By then, the RCMP were looking into the disappearance of Gerald Foisy and Shirley Rosette. This is perhaps the greatest mystery still surrounding the tragedy. They were in the cafeteria at closing time, 11:30 PM, sharing a

• • • • • • • • • • • •

14 WCAT Decision 39–41.
15 WCAT Decision, 41.
16 WCAT Decision, 42.
17 WCAT Decision, 43.
18 WCAT Decision, 45.
19 WCAT Decision, 50.

meal with another passenger. Fifty minutes later they were nowhere to be found. The most common assumption is that they were aboard the ship, presumably sleeping, and we somehow missed them in our search. That is exceedingly difficult to believe. They had taken a cabin and every cabin that had been let was searched at least once. They did not have a car, so it would make no sense for them to be on the car deck. Most passengers were woken by the shock of the grounding and had left their cabins before the crew made their check,[20] so it's unlikely they slept through the shock of the grounding, followed by the half-hour commotion of the evacuation, with crew members searching every likely space and calling out. It has been suggested that they might have been injured or knocked unconscious in some hidden space—but the impact was not that forceful and didn't seriously injure anyone else. And it's highly unlikely it would have knocked both of them out for all the thirty-plus minutes of the evacuation. It has been suggested they were on an outside deck, where the impact caused them to be thrown overboard, but all the passenger areas were surrounded by high, sturdy railings that were not affected by the grounding. There were several eyewitness accounts claiming to have seen them alive after the sinking, and for a time I held out hope that they might have made their own escape, but with the passage of time that hope faded. The mystery remains. Initially the Mounties' involvement in their disappearance was described as a missing persons investigation, but within a few days of the sinking I was told it was a criminal investigation. I was interviewed by the RCMP numerous times.[21]

There were also several lawsuits, the first of which was filed on March 27, 2006, by Alexander and Maria Kotai, passengers who had been carrying valuable property on the ship in the process of moving house. This was followed by a lawsuit from the family of Gerald Foisy on May 11, 2006. The family of Shirley Rosette filed their lawsuit on July 29, 2007. The suit filed by the Kotais was a class-action suit; more than forty passengers eventually joined in. I was named as a defendant in every one of these suits, along with BC Ferries and Karl Lilgert. Jack Buchan told me that, based on past practice, he expected BC Ferries would offer a joint defence. However, that was not to be.

· · · · · · · · · · · ·

20   TSB Report, 9.

21   Corporal Pacholuk of the RCMP assuaged my fears at the beginning of the first interview by telling me that they were not gunning for me, and that he felt it was an honour just to be sitting in the same room as me.

As soon as I was named in a lawsuit, Jack found another lawyer to represent me in order to avoid any potential conflict of interest between Karl and me. Nils Daugulis, a senior maritime lawyer with the Vancouver firm Bull, Housser, and Tupper, took over during the summer of 2006 and represented me throughout the remainder of the TSB and RCMP investigations as well as through the lawsuits.

FIRED

In January 2007 we were still waiting for the TSB final report as well as the final report from the DI. January 11 was a cold but sunny winter day. I was driving through the Kootenay town of Creston, on my way home from visiting my parents, when my cell phone rang. I pulled onto the shoulder of the road, by the old grain elevators, to answer. Glen Schwartz, BC Ferries' executive vice president (human resources), was on the line. He asked affably how I was doing.

Modern corporatese is a language of clichés, idioms, and innuendos. At first I thought Schwartz was speaking of a plan to ease my way back to work. Instead, he was firing me.

Standing on the side of the road, cell phone in hand, I was in a familiar place that suddenly felt very strange and a long way from anywhere.

I drove on to the home of an old friend and shipmate who put me up for the night. When I got home the next day, a Friday afternoon, I was still at a complete loss. I decided to call my lawyer. My legal defence insurance did not cover wrongful dismissal cases, so I was counting on Nils's good favour to help me with some kind of advice. I doubted he would even be in the office on a late Friday afternoon, but he was there. Over the next few months I learned just how hard these lawyers work and what long hours they put in.

Nils told me there was a large labour department at his firm and that he would call back on Monday. As good as his word, he called me early Monday morning. With him was labour lawyer Howard Ehrlich, who would become my champion and hero.

Howard listened to me and asked a couple of questions. A few days later he called to say he had reached the conclusion that BC Ferries had fired me for raising safety issues.

"Think about it," he said. "The only things that happened between their taking you into management and their firing you were: 1) you attended a seminar; 2) you sailed as master for one week; 3) the ship sank; 4) you were interviewed by the company's inquiry and you raised some safety concerns.

"They had no complaints about your performance during that one week, and they placed no blame on you for the sinking so, by process of elimination, the only thing you did that they didn't like was that you raised safety concerns." Howard told me not to get worked up, and he began the process of building his case.

In the meantime, Schwartz's phone call was followed by a letter dated January 15, 2007. The reason given for "negotiating" my termination was the "company's operational and staff requirements."[22] This was in spite of the fact that BC Ferries was actively recruiting masters at the time, as well as lowering its standards for masters and mates (with the intention of fast-tracking potential masters). In the *Victoria Times Colonist* of October 25, 2006, Cindy Harnett had reported:

> In the face of a labour shortage, more retirements, and a new fleet of three Super-C ships coming into service, the corporation has dropped its "restrictive" certification standards to help junior officers advance through the ranks faster, said George Capacci, B.C. Ferries vice-president of fleet operations.
>
> Capacci said he won't be losing any sleep over the situation. "These are people who are very close to getting a master licence," said Capacci. "Let's be serious. That's still someone who's done six to eight years at sea."[23]

Howard and I filed a request under the Freedom of Information Act, asking BC Ferries for every document that concerned me personally. It took more than ten months, and we had to file a complaint with the Privacy Commissioner, but thanks to Howard's tireless efforts to pursue my rights, we did succeed in getting from BC Ferries more than the two meagre documents they initially supplied. Some of these documents were crucial to establishing my case. For example, one document was the copy

· · · · · · · · · · · ·

22 WCAT Decision, 65.

23 On April 8, 2008, Sandra McCulloch of the *Times Colonist* reported "B.C. Ferries continues to bring Captains out of retirement to work on a contractual basis."

of an email sent to Capacci in July 2006 by one of the managers. It concerned a request I had made for some job-related training. The email read, "I have been stonewalling this request, but what do I tell him." Capacci's answer was not in the material disclosed under the *Personal Information Protection Act*, but the word "stonewalling" was a telling descriptor of the company's initial strategy to counter my fight to save my career.

On January 10, 2008, Howard filed a discriminatory action complaint with the Workers' Compensation Board (WCB).[24] He based my case on Section 151 of the *Workers' Compensation Act*, which forbids an employer from discriminating in any way against an employee who has given information concerning safety or occupational health.

In his summary of facts, Howard noted that the *Queen of the North* sank due to no fault of mine; that David Hahn, president and CEO of BC Ferries, had commended me and my crew, in press releases, company newsletters, and emails, for our actions during the sinking; and that after raising safety concerns at the DI, the panel had asked me twice why I had taken the job of exempt master and also asked if I still wanted to work for BC Ferries. He also brought up the fact that BC Ferries had given the "company's operational and staff requirements" as the reason for letting me go, even though the company was advertising for exempt masters at the same time and dropping its certification standards to help junior officers advance through the ranks more quickly. Howard argued that my firing would send a message to employees that reporting a safety concern could result in the threat of dismissal.

In March 2008, Howard and I attended a mediation session with representatives of BC Ferries, which had been arranged by the WCB. The BC Ferries representatives charged me with trying to duck out of my responsibilities and being interested only in self-preservation. They claimed that by accepting the company's invitation to bring my lawyer to the Divisional Inquiry, I was saying that I was not a member of management and, again, only showing an interest in self-preservation.

After the mediation session, Howard proceeded with the complaint to the WCB. It was a meticulous and comprehensive work. He designed it to win, and it did.

On July 21, 2008, the WCB case officer released her decision, which

. . . .
24 AKA WorkSafeBC.

found that I had been fired for raising safety issues: "Simply put, the case officer found that the worker's raising safety concerns ... during the DI proceedings played a role in the employer deciding he was not a management team player and thus terminating his employment."[25]

BC Ferries appealed the WCB decision.

In November 2009, six months after reporting for work, I took command of the *Northern Adventure*. Between then and March 16, 2010, I took three regular two-week shifts, Christmas included, as master.

And between the day I reported for duty in May and the day I took command of the ship, I attended my hearings at the Workers' Compensation Appeal Tribunal, spread over ten days in June, August, September, and November. Howard Ehrlich continued to represent me in his fierce and meticulous manner. It seemed to me that he destroyed every argument, caught BC Ferries in half-truths and untruths, and left no doubt as to the justice of my cause.

Driving me home to my friends' house in Vancouver one day, Howard turned to me and asked, "Do you know why your case resonates for me?"

"Why?"

"When I was growing up I was bullied *every* day. And I will be *damned* if I will sit by and watch this kind of abuse of power."

On March 12, 2010, I was on board the *Northern Adventure* in Prince Rupert when Howard phoned me with news of the WCAT decision. The tribunal had overturned the WCB decision. I had lost. Howard was completely flabbergasted. It seemed as if the members of the tribunal had not even been in the same room when Howard had done his best to demolish BC Ferries' case.

I knew I would be fired. BC Ferries waited until I had completed the voyage from Prince Rupert to Port Hardy before officially notifying me. The company apparently didn't want to have its service disrupted by firing me—even though its vice president of fleet operations claimed he had lost confidence in me as a master.[26]

. . . .

25 WCAT Decision, 7.

26 WCAT Decision, 30–31.

CHAPTER 5

THE CRIMINALIZATION
OF A SEAFARER

In what will undoubtedly prove to be a seminal case in Canadian maritime law, for the first time, Canadian authorities have laid criminal charges against a crew member in connection with a fatal marine collision.

—Graham Walker, Borden, Ladner, Gervais LLP,
March 18, 2010.

ON MARCH 17, 2010—LESS THAN A WEEK AFTER I LOST THE APPEAL, and almost four years after the sinking—the RCMP arrested Karl Lilgert and charged him with criminal negligence causing death. He was released on bail and on condition that he have no contact with me and with fifteen listed crew members. He was also barred from operating a vessel in a professional capacity. The charge of criminal negligence carries a maximum penalty of life imprisonment.

Within days of the sinking, some observers expressed strong opinions about what happened to the *Queen of the North,* and placed the blame squarely on Lilgert. One of these observers was retired captain Lewis Glentworth, formerly of the *Queen of Prince Rupert* and the *Queen of the North,* who spoke to several newspaper reporters in the week after the sinking.

The last voyage of the Queen of the North has haunted Lew Glentworth for the past two nights.
Lying awake, staring into the darkness, the retired

British Columbia ferry captain with 30 years experience on the northern run has played over in his mind the harrowing stories told to him by the crew members he worked with until recently.

And he has come to a shocking conclusion.[1]

His "shocking conclusion" was that human error, not mechanical failure, caused the sinking.[2] "People have suggested perhaps there was an equipment failure. Well, yeah, there may have been an equipment failure, but everything wouldn't have quit at once. You wouldn't have had two radars, the GPS, and an electronic charting system all go down at the same time."[3] And, he told another reporter, "if the malfunction was that irreconcilable, then the ship should have been stopped."[4]

Glentworth said that he had been talking to some of the crew members, whom he had sailed with before he retired in September 2005, and "What I am told by people who were on the scene was that that ship went along the shore, almost parallel to the shore, and systematically ripped open the bottom going at full speed.

"I'm also told ... after the ship glanced along the beach, it then came to rest on a rock that protrudes just from the beach ... The rock is called Gil Rock. Had the ship not hung up on that rock then she would have continued into deep water and simply sunk and there would have been major loss of life. The fact that she hung up on the rock allowed them the time to get those people off."[5]

Actually, he was off by nearly a mile. The *Queen of the North* never touched Gil Rock. She hit at Juan Point, more than half a mile from the

• • • • • • • • • • • •

1   Mark Hume, "How the Queen Lost Its Way," *Globe and Mail,* March 25, 2006, http://www.theglobeandmail.com/news/national/how-the-queen-lost-its-way/article 1097088/

2   Dirk Meissner, "Doomed Ferry on Autopilot at Time of Sinking, Sources Say," *Globe and Mail,* March 27, 2006, http://www.theglobeandmail.com/news/national /doomed-ferry-on-autopilot-at-time-of-sinking-sources-say/article1096745/

3   Hume, "How the Queen Lost Its Way."

4   Dirk Meissner, "Ferry Union President Blasts 'Armchair' Navigators," Canadian Press, March 28, 2006.

5   Hume, "How the Queen Lost Its Way."

rock, and she did continue into deep water. It was her own buoyancy and stability that kept her afloat long enough for us to abandon ship.

I'm also not sure how he reached the conclusion the ship was travelling "at full speed." According to the TSB Report the actual speed at time of grounding was 17.5 knots, which was no more than three-quarters of her top speed.

And I don't know how he was able to dismiss the possibility of equipment failure so quickly. The *Queen of the North* had a documented record of equipment failure, including total steering failures that could never be explained (one occurred in August 2005; incident reports were filed), as well as failures of the autopilot that were also never explained. Critical equipment malfunctioning at a key moment could well have made the difference between clearing and striking Gil Island. For Glentworth to have ruled this out at such an early stage seems something of a rush to judgment.

Eight months later, Glentworth signed an affidavit on behalf of the passengers who had filed a lawsuit against BC Ferries, Karl Lilgert, Karen Briker, and me in which he declared that "whatever was taking place on the bridge at the time of the sinking was equivalent to an abandonment of the responsibilities of navigation."[6]

By the time Lilgert came to trial, the declarations of various expert witnesses, pundits, and armchair sailors had been so widely publicized that it seemed to be almost universally accepted that the accident was caused by negligence. People who were not there had made categorical statements about the state of the weather, about the state of the equipment, about the ship hanging up on Gil Rock (it didn't), and about the precise damage that had been done to the ship (as if they had swum down 1,400 feet/427 metres, cleared away the silt that buried the hull, and examined it).

Many writers of letters to the editor and callers to talk shows expressed disbelief that a ferry following the same course it had safely navigated thousands of times could come to grief at all, especially as the result of as gross a navigational blunder as the *Queen of the North* had seemingly made. This attitude is perhaps understandable in non-mariners. Experienced mariners know that vessels on scheduled runs do not have the luxury of

· · · · · · · · · · · ·

6   "Queen of the North Affidavits Allege Recklessness," CBC News, November 20, 2006, http://www.cbc.ca/news/canada/british-columbia/queen-of-the-north-affidavits -allege-recklessness-1.609166

choosing when to sail; they have to be out there every day except in the most extreme conditions, and they are out there so much that they are more likely than other vessels to be involved in freak occurrences—perfect storms of weather, traffic, equipment failure, or poor judgment that the more occasional seaman might never face. In this sense, highly repetitive navigation carries with it a special risk: if anything can go wrong, sooner or later it will.

The most malicious rumour was that the two people on the bridge, Fourth Mate Karl Lilgert and Quartermaster Karen Briker, were "having sex." I would guess that anyone who has heard of the sinking has heard that rumour. *Maclean's* magazine called it "perhaps the best-known rumour in B.C."[7] A dismaying number of people believe it to this day.

Michel Huot, one of the ten prosecutors at Lilgert's trial, emphasized it. Huot accused Lilgert of relieving the second mate, Keven Hilton, early so he could be alone with Briker on the bridge. "The relationship the two of you shared," Huot said, "the attraction was powerful enough that whether it was sexual activity or an argument or a discussion coming out of the breakup of the relationship, that's what occupied your attention that night, not navigating the vessel."[8] The fact that the prosecution couldn't decide whether to accuse the pair of making love or making war shows just how little evidence they had to suggest anything untoward had taken place between them at all.

The only two people present—Lilgert and Briker—testified that they had merely engaged in sporadic conversation during the watch. It would be very strange if they hadn't. If crew members working long shifts on a bridge don't speak to each other, it indicates something amiss with the working relationship. Briker testified that she had been showing some fellow crew members "paint swatches she was considering for the walls of a home she had recently purchased. Hours later, when Briker and Lilgert found themselves alone together on the bridge, Briker said the subject of the house came up again." Lilgert reportedly said, "I didn't know you were

• • • • • • • • • • • • •

7   Nancy MacDonald, "B.C. Jury Convicts Karl Lilgert," *Maclean's*, May 13, 2013, http://www.macleans.ca/news/canada/b-c-jury-convicts-karl-lilgert-in-fatal-ferry-sinking/

8   Tyler Harbottle, "Karl Lilgert Trial: Sex, Argument May Have Distracted Officer, Says Crown," Canadian Press, April 25, 2013, http://www.huffingtonpost.ca/2013/04/25/karl-lilgert-trial-sex-ferry-sinking_n_3156872.html

buying a house."[9] This was played up by the Crown as evidence of hot passion, although it could just as easily be seen as evidence the pair were no longer close. Their own evidence was that they had had a brief affair in the past, but that it had been casual and was over. It may not have come up but for an unknown informant who passed the rumour on to the RCMP.[10] When the prosecution brought the matter up at Lilgert's trial, a Canadian Press reporter described it as "the accusation the court had been waiting to hear."[11] Prosecutor Robert Wright aired details of the affair when the trial started in January 2013, but, as newspapers reported, "didn't say how the affair fits into the Crown's theory about what happened that night."[12]

Nobody seemed to give serious consideration to the fact that the bridge of a moving ship is subject to constant, unannounced intrusion, making it one of the most unsuitable venues imaginable for any kind of intimate behaviour, or that it would be bizarrely out of character for a veteran seaman entrusted with the conduct of a BC Ferries flagship to risk his career, his ship, and the lives of all on board, including his own, for a moment of foolish indulgence. Certainly those who knew Lilgert as a responsible shipmate who took great pride in his professionalism find it unthinkable. But the salacious innuendo hung over the incident and the trial, becoming an unacknowledged lens through which other facts were viewed—by the public, by the press, by the investigators, and quite possibly by the judge and jury. For years afterward, whenever a ferry was late, it was common to hear wags say, "They must be having sex on the bridge again." Every formal hearing, from BC Ferries' own Divisional Inquiry to the Workers Compensation Board Appeal Tribunal to the Supreme Court, felt justified in making assumptions about Lilgert's being "distracted" and

. . . .

9   "Ex-Lover Testifies in B.C. Ferry Sinking Trial," Canadian Press, March 5, 2013, http://www.cbc.ca/news/canada/british-columbia/ex-lover-testifies-in-b-c-ferry-sinking-trial-1.1317400

10   Michael Smyth, "Sex on the Ferry Myth Doesn't Die: Queen of the North Victims Deserve the Truth," Vancouver *Province*, October 7, 2007.

11   Harbottle, "Karl Lilgert Trial: Sex, Argument May Have Distracted Officer, Says Crown."

12   James Keller, "Karl Lilgert On Trial for BC Ferry Queen of the North Sinking," Canadian Press, January 17, 2013, http://www.huffingtonpost.ca/2013/01/17/karl-lilgert-bc-ferry-queen-of-the-north-sinking_n_2493214.html

"not doing his job."[13] In this way the rumour may have been as effective a prosecution weapon as any smoking gun. By the time Lilgert took the stand in late April 2013, the sensationalistic "fooling around on the bridge" narrative was so deeply rooted it was extremely difficult for a more mundane and plausible explanation to be appreciated.

In his testimony, Lilgert said "that he decided not to alter course at Sainty Point like normal but chose to delay for three minutes because a tugboat towing a log boom and another vessel—which the Crown has called 'the phantom vessel'—were in the area."[14] He spent several minutes trying to locate this ship using radar, and testified that he did make two small course changes: "the first came three minutes after Sainty Point at the end of Grenville Channel—a key course change necessary to avoid Gil Island, while the second alteration was made to adjust for the effect the wind was having on the vessel's course." (The report of the Divisional Inquiry also notes that Briker "remembered making one or possibly two small course alterations as directed by the 4/0 … after taking over the watch."[15])

> "My decision was to go deeper into Wright Sound for about three minutes and then alter course," Lilgert said.
>
> When asked why he chose three minutes as a number, Lilgert said "three minutes wouldn't put me in any danger of Gil Island and would allow me enough room between the Queen of the North and the tug."
>
> Then the wind started to pick up, Lilgert said. The rain got harder.
>
> "I could hear it against the windows," he said.
>
> He made the course alteration at the three minute mark as he had planned.
>
> But when he turned on an electronic chart to check

· · · · · · · · · · · ·

13   James Keller, "Karl Lilgert Sentenced to Four Years in Jail," Canadian Press, June 24, 2013, http://www.huffingtonpost.ca/2013/06/24/karl-lilgert-trial-sentence_n_3488798 .html

14   Harbottle, "Karl Lilgert Trial: Sex, Argument May Have Distracted Officer, Says Crown."

15   Divisional Inquiry, 14.

his course, Lilgert said he noticed the ship was further north than he thought it was.

"I thought, hmm, we are being set pretty good with this wind. We were getting further aport. We were travelling forward but we were getting sucked aport," Lilgert said.

He said he wanted to allow for a safe distance between the vessel he identified on the radar and the Queen of the North.

To make up for the wind's effect, Lilgert said he decided to alter the course to the starboard—towards Gil Island.

Lilgert said his plan was to sail past the island at three cables—or about half a kilometre—which would take the Queen of the North between Gil Island and the boat Lilgert saw on the radar.

When pressed by the Crown, who said Lilgert made a course alteration that was taking the ferry on a direct course to Gil Island, Lilgert quipped back, "I wasn't steering it to Gil Island. I was three cables off. Three cables is perfect. It's what we use going through McKay Reach."

Lilgert admitted that at that point he was not able to see Gil Island, but said "I did not believe for a moment that we are going to be closer than three cables to Gil Island."

But they were closer. "I was so certain that I was three cables off," Lilgert said, "I was shocked in realizing that that wasn't where I was."[16]

When told by the court the electronic data didn't show course alterations, Lilgert said he did not understand why.[17]

Briker had testified earlier, and Canadian Press reported:

The ship was on autopilot, and at some point, Lilgert

16 Tyler Harbottle, "Karl Lilgert Trial: BC Ferry Officer 'Absolutely Horrified' Before Crash," Canadian Press, April 23, 2013, http://www.huffingtonpost.ca/2013/04/23/karl -lilgert-trial-bc-ferry_n_3141662.html

17 Harbottle, "Karl Lilgert Trial: Sex, Argument May Have Distracted Officer, Says Crown."

ordered Briker to enter a large course correction into the system ... Before she could make the change, Briker saw trees through a window that were illuminated by the ferry's lights.

"I then remember hearing him say something like, 'Oh my God,' or, 'Oh no,'" said Briker. "He then ordered me to turn off the autopilot and I told him that I didn't know how."

...

Briker was a casual employee, and she had said she hadn't worked on the bridge of that ship for nearly a year ...

Shortly after, Briker said she overheard Lilgert speaking with another officer.

"I heard him say, 'I'm sorry, I'm sorry, I was trying to go around a fishing boat. We hit a squall and the radar screen had whited out.'"[18]

Second Mate Keven Hilton also testified that Lilgert mentioned another boat, saying "Karl said he was giving the other boat some room," although Hilton also "told the court there was nothing to indicate there had been another boat in the nearby vicinity or anything more than the usual rain at the time."[19]

The media gave any mention of another boat short shrift, quickly returning to the prosecution's narrative, which said that Lilgert was distracted from his navigation duties because he and his former lover—the only other person on the bridge when the *Queen of the North* crashed—were either arguing about their breakup or having sex. Lilgert was convicted on May 13, 2013, and sentenced to four years in jail on June 24, 2013. Even Judge Sunni Stromberg-Stein in her sentencing decision said she thought Lilgert's relationship with quartermaster Karen Briker was a significant

• • • • • • • • • • •

18   James Keller, "Karl Lilgert Trial: Karen Briker Wasn't Trained On Autopilot," Canadian Press, May 3, 2013, http://www.huffingtonpost.ca/2013/03/05/karl-lilgert -trial-karen-briker-autopilot-training_n_2812881.html

19   Tamsyn Burgmann, "Karl Lilgert Trial: Navigator Blames Other Boat, Visibility for BC Ferry Crash," Canadian Press, February 19, 2013, http://www.huffingtonpost. ca/2013/02/19/karl-lilgert-trial-navigator-blames-boat-visibility-bc-ferry-crash_n _2718578.html

factor in the crash. "Clearly, he was distracted by personal issues related to his relationship with Ms. Briker," said Stromberg-Stein. "I do not need to speculate on what Mr. Lilgert was doing on the bridge that night. I know what he was not doing. He was not doing his job."[20]

This finding may have been the best outcome for an otherwise disastrous event for BC Ferries. To some extent it deflected blame away from the company and onto replaceable employees. It gave the travelling public some reassurance that the problem had been dealt with.

Another way of looking at the incident, and one it is safe to say BC Ferries would not favour, was that "given the state of the company's safety practices and protocols, the fleet was an 'accident waiting to happen'" and that "systemic problems that affected the whole fleet … might have been the cause, or one of the causes, of the sinking of the *Queen of the North*."[21] This view was held by none other than BC Ferries' own director of safety, health and environment, Captain Darin Bowland.

Bowland's case is instructive. A master mariner and maritime safety expert who spent eleven years with Royal Caribbean Cruise Lines, most recently as captain of the luxury liner *Radiance of the Seas*, Bowland had been headhunted by BC Ferries, joining the company in February 2006. According to an affidavit entered in the Supreme Court of British Columbia on September 17, 2006, Bowland had seen enough within three weeks to inform senior management that the company's Occupational Health and Safety organization was in disarray, producing a negative effect on the International Safety Management (ISM) system at BC Ferries that could raise liability issues for company directors and officers. Bowland arranged a visit between senior officers and Chris Clack, BC Ferries' director, operational safety and audit with responsibility for ISM, who, Bowland said, confirmed that the ISM system at BC Ferries was "broken." Bowland subsequently compiled all of the outstanding safety deficiencies he had detected at BC Ferries into one document, totalling "over 800 deficiencies—or safety problems that had been identified but not fixed." According to his affidavit, his insights were not met with great enthusiasm by head office.

· · · · · · · · · · · ·

20   Keller, "Karl Lilgert Sentenced to Four Years in Jail."

21   Affidavit #1 of Darin Bowland, sworn September 17, 2006, in the Supreme Court of British Columbia, No. s-063817 (Vancouver Registry), http://www.cbc.ca/bc/news/061019_affidavit.pdf

At one point, Bowland said, Executive Vice President Mike Corrigan sent him word "that he did not want me trying to make changes so quickly." "My recommendations were generally met with indifference," Bowland said, adding that he thought one of his most pressing concerns—the urgent need for Bridge Resource Management (BRM) training for the crews of the ferries and a position to oversee such training—was implemented after the sinking of the *Queen of the North*.

Part of Bowland's contractual duties was to investigate accidents and conduct Divisional Inquiries. Nevertheless, when word came of the sinking, he "was not part of the initial accident response team that the BC Ferries executive team sent to Prince Rupert." He was sent later to conduct the Divisional Inquiry but, as mentioned previously, resigned after coming to the conclusion BC Ferries would not support his continuing the inquiry. BC Ferries put out a press release saying he had resigned for "personal reasons," but he responded, "The primary reason that I felt compelled to leave BC Ferries was that its commitment to safety was not what it had represented to me during the pre-employment interviews and discussions we had, and in my employment contract. Rather, BC Ferries failed to support my initiatives to improve the safety for its employees and for the public as a whole ... I left because of my negative experiences with BC Ferries' approach to safety and what had transpired in Prince Rupert ... Bottom line—the company scares me and I am not willing to carry on within the current culture and organization."[22]

After Bowland resigned, Trafford Taylor, BC Ferries' vice president, operations, took over as chairman of the Divisional Inquiry and oversaw a finding that, while it didn't exonerate BC Ferries, placed the blame primarily on the fourth mate, saying he "failed to make a necessary course alteration or verify such alteration was made in accordance with pre-established Fleet Routing Directives and good seamanship."[23]

I have to agree with Captain Bowland that "systemic problems ... might have been the cause, or one of the causes, of the sinking of the *Queen of the North*."

. . . .

22   Ibid.

23   Divisional Inquiry, 24.

CHAPTER 6

WHAT HAPPENED

WHEN I WAS ASKED AT THE DIVISIONAL INQUIRY WHAT HAD HAPPENED to cause the loss of the *Queen of the North*, I said that I didn't know. BC Ferries cited this, in their defence of my firing, as evidence that I lacked a properly managerial attitude, but at the time it was true.[1] I knew nothing about the cause of the grounding, and I was not willing to make up what I didn't know. I was criticized for failing to interrogate the officer of the watch,[2] but the only time I spoke to Lilgert was when we were both preoccupied with the urgent business of evacuating the ship's company, and that did not allow for discussion of anything but the task at hand. In the period immediately following the sinking he was in no mental condition to discuss the accident, and after I was helicoptered away from Hartley Bay, I had no access to him. It was not until after his trial for criminal negligence causing death, where I testified, that I was able to put together a full picture of what happened that fateful night. Based on my knowledge of the ship, the conditions, the participants, and all the evidence that has come to light, this is my best attempt to reconstruct the incident. I apologize in advance to anyone who bought this book hoping for confirmation of lurid rumours about sex or drugs on the bridge. The probable reality is, as usual, much less sensational.

. . . .

1   WCAT Decision, 30–31, 50–52.

2   WCAT Decision, 52: "Captain C[apacci] testified that if he had been a Master who had watched his ship sink he would have asked the 2/O or 4/O 'what the hell happened—what did you do to my ship?'"

When the *Queen of the North* reached the southern end of Grenville Channel, Fourth Mate Karl Lilgert used the electronic chart system (ECS) to find the expected time of arrival (ETA) for the next calling-in point (Kingcome Point), then dimmed its screen to prevent it from degrading his night vision. He called Prince Rupert Traffic and gave them the ETA.

As he left Grenville Channel, Lilgert entered Wright Sound, a section of the main thoroughfare we know as the Inside Passage. This is not some abandoned stretch of highway; it is the usual route for marine traffic travelling between Seattle in the south and Juneau in the north. Wright Sound is the junction of seven main channels that are in use year-round. Marine traffic is a constant concern for mariners, and it is usual to encounter other vessels here in any season, in any weather, and at any time of the day or night. Lilgert was aware of the tug *Castle Lake* coming down Verney Passage with a tow of logs bound for Prince Rupert. He was aware of the fishing vessel *Lone Star*, which was ahead of him and travelling in the same direction as the *Queen of the North*. Lilgert said he could see its stern light and the associated target on his radar screen. He used radar to track this vessel and predict its further movement. He later testified that there was also an unknown vessel ahead of him, no doubt too small for the requirement to check in with the vessel traffic system.

It was at about this time that the *Queen of the North* encountered the squall—high wind, heavy rain—and, with it, reduced visibility. As the rain increased in intensity, the resulting "clutter" on the radar screen obliterated the unknown vessel's echo and it became lost.

Various controls and techniques are available to reduce the clutter on a radar screen. Their proper use is a highly developed skill acquired through education and experience. If the operator has exhausted the full range of these controls and techniques and still cannot reduce the clutter to an acceptable level—one that allows him and the Automatic Radar Plotting Aid (ARPA) to track the desired target—his next option is to go from the X-band radar—the one normally used for navigation under most conditions—to the S-band radar. The S-band uses a longer wavelength with a lower frequency, less susceptible to the unwanted echoes of rain and sea. There being no free lunches at sea, the S-band radar presents a less precise radar picture, sometimes described as "softer" or "mushy." The displayed images of the land and other vessels are much less sharp. Again, highly developed skill must be brought to bear. I stated in my testimony at Lilgert's trial that, in my opinion, the *Queen of the North*'s radars were third rate. The S-band unit was new, and we had had no opportunity to try it in foul weather. Theoretically, it should have performed better in foul weather than the X-band, but given the substandard performance of its X-band sister, that is not saying much.

With the unknown vessel still out there, it became a priority for Lilgert to find it. When the squall hit, the *Lone Star* had, of course, taken shelter well out of the ferry's path; the other boat may have done the same thing, but without a readable radar image there was no way for Lilgert to know this. All he knew was that he had lost its position, and until he located it again he could not be sure he wasn't running it down.

Avoiding small craft is a constant preoccupation of every navigator on the coast. One of the more notorious incidents involving BC Ferries occurred in 1985 when the *Queen of Cowichan* collided with a smaller boat near Horseshoe Bay, killing three people on the boat, and no officer wanted to risk a repeat of that scenario. Since he could not locate the unknown vessel visually, Lilgert needed to find it on radar. Until he did, it would make no sense for him to alter his ship's course toward that vessel's last known position. Wright Sound is a relatively wide open body of water. With plenty of room and a good bit of time, something like nine to ten minutes before he would be nearing Gil Island, there was no urgency to alter course at the exact point where he had planned. In his testimony during his criminal trial, Lilgert stated that he did not *miss* his alteration of course: he delayed it. The prosecution ridiculed the idea that Lilgert might have been trying to avoid an unidentified vessel in Wright Sound, calling it a "phantom vessel" and suggesting Lilgert invented it to cover up for his alleged negligence, but several people, including me, reported seeing something that could have been a boat's light. When I first came to the bridge I saw a steady white light that looked like the stern light of a small boat heading away from us, and I gave testimony to this effect. Passenger Edward Kennedy, "who recounted many details of the night with precision," testified that he "saw what he thought was a 'masthead light' of a ship travelling from east to west near Sainty Point ... while he was standing on the deck waiting to board a lifeboat ... He said the vessel appeared to be travelling at a speed befitting a fishing boat, but not as slow as a tugboat."[3]

. . . .

3   Tyler Harbottle, "Karl Lilgert Trial: Sex, Argument May Have Distracted Officer, Says Crown," Canadian Press, April 25, 2013, http://www.huffingtonpost.ca/2013/04/25/karl-lilgert-trial-sex-ferry-sinking_n_3156872.html

And, yes, we know that Lilgert conversed with the person he was on watch with.

That is the extent of what we know. Everything else is supposition. His testimony, that he delayed altering the course and then gave Karen Briker a command to alter course, is completely believable and is actually the most likely explanation for what happened.

The TSB Report stated that he was "likely" distracted by the conversation, even though they said it was "intermittent": so that is all supposition. The judge said that he was "clearly" distracted by the conversation: supposition squared. Expert witnesses Lew Glentworth and Andrew Flotre implied that he abandoned his duties. The prosecution said that he was negligent. I say that the very opposite of that is a far more likely explanation: that he became so absorbed in solving the problem of locating and avoiding the unknown vessel that he lost sight of the otherwise simple problem of navigating across Wright Sound. He lost track of time. If you are moving when that happens, you lose track of distance.

In its report of another, unrelated, marine incident, the TSB presented this case:

> It is known that, when people find themselves in a situation where they must solve a problem to which no rules apply and a new solution or plan must be formulated, there is a tendency to frame the problem as a choice between gains and losses. With respect to losses, people are biased toward choosing the risky loss—even if it is potentially more disastrous—rather than the certain loss.[4]

Karl Lilgert testified that in order to avoid the vessel ahead, he could not steer the direct course that would normally be taken, and so he set a course which was to starboard of it, a course that would leave the other

· · · · · · · · · · · ·

4   Transportation Safety Board, "Tug Girding and Capsizing: Tug *North Arm Venture* While Towing the Barge *North Arm Express*, Entrance to Sechelt Rapids, British Columbia, 19 July 2009," Marine Investigation Report M09W0141 (http://www.tsb.gc.ca /eng/rapports-reports/marine/2009/m09w0141/m09w0141.asp), 12, citing T. Gilovich, D. Griffon, and D. Kahneman, eds., *Heuristics and Biases: The Psychology of Intuitive Judgement* (Cambridge Press, 2002).

vessel on his port hand, and Gil Island on his starboard hand, clearing Gil Island by 3 cables (3/10 of a nautical mile or 0.56 kilometres).[5]

Presuming that the *Queen of the North* passed Sainty Point at a distance of 0.5 nautical miles or 0.93 kilometres (a normal passing distance), then the course to clear Gil Island by 3 cables would have been 3.4 degrees to port of Juan Point, Gil Island's left-hand edge. To visualize this, point your imaginary ship directly at Juan Point (5 nautical miles/9.3 kilometres away) and then bring it to the left 3.4 degrees.

You will notice that 3.4 degrees and 0.3 nautical miles are pretty small numbers.

Lilgert reasoned that this would be a safe margin, because we pass Trivett Point and Kingcome Point in McKay Reach at that distance. But it doesn't take much to make that 0.3-mile buffer disappear. For the ship to move laterally 0.3 miles over a period of fourteen minutes (the time it takes to travel from Sainty Point to Gil Island) requires a lateral speed of 1.2 knots. The ship had already encountered one squall that night, with winds gusting to 30 knots or more,[6] and if the wind in Wright Sound was anything like Lilgert said it was, it could easily account for that kind of leeway (the lateral movement of the ship caused by the wind).[7] Ships like the *Queen of the North* make a lot of leeway due to the high superstructure. Seamen say "she has a lot of sail area."

When a strong low-pressure weather system reaches the BC coast, the prevailing wind is south-easterly, but locally the wind direction is shaped by the channels as it funnels through them. Seven channels enter into Wright Sound, creating what Environment Canada calls "chaotic conditions."[8] When the *Queen of the North* exited Grenville Channel into Wright Sound, the wind whistling through Lewis Passage on her starboard side

. . . .

5   A cable is 1/10 of a nautical mile.

6   TSB Report, 12.

7   It doesn't take any "abnormality" in terms of wind or current, as one witness described it, to put the ship off course that amount. Rebekah Funk, "Karl Lilgert Trial: Safety Checks Missed by Crew, Says Mariner," Canadian Press, April 11, 2013, http://www.huffingtonpost.ca/2013/04/11/karl-lilgert-trial-bc-ferry-safety-checks_n_3064039.html

8   Environment Canada, Atmospheric Environment Service, *Marine Weather Hazards Manual—West Coast*, 3rd ed. (Ottawa: Minister of Public Works and Government Services, 1999), 112.

would have exerted a strong push, and the ship would have made leeway to port. Lilgert testified that he was surprised to find how much the ship was moving to the port of her course. To compensate for this push, he made a small alteration of course to starboard, into the wind, to counteract it. When the *Queen of the North* drew abeam of the north end of Gil Island, the wind funnelling through Lewis Passage would no longer have been acting on her. She would now be under the influence of the wind blowing up Wright Sound. This wind would be more from ahead or affecting her port side. If Lilgert was still aiming to pass 3 cables off Gil Island, the course adjustment he had applied would now be moving him away from the wind and toward the Gil Island shore.

When the electronic chart computer was salvaged from the wreck, it did not show the ship's course as a straight line from Sainty Point to Juan Point, but as a zigzag track that approximated a straight line. Close inspection revealed that the zigs and zags deflected up to 4 degrees from the average. The zigs and zags could have been the result of the small alterations which Lilgert claimed to have made; they could have been the effect of the gusting wind; they could have been a combination. The fact that the ship did not travel in a straight line opened up a number of possibilities that were not given serious consideration at trial.

The current alone could have been sufficient to push the ship onto Gil Island, given the small margin the navigator had allowed. In Wright Sound the current is *always* setting onto Juan Point, due largely to the outflowing current from Douglas Channel, which is driven by the wind, the flow from the Kitimat River, and the forces of the tide. Weather conditions alone can increase or decrease the current by as much as 1 knot.[9] That is all that would have been needed.

Don't forget that one degree of difference in the course would have been sufficient to miss the island. Even with only a little wind and current, a one-degree offset can disappear: it is not unrealistic to have a half-degree gyro error, a half-degree error between the gyro and its repeater, a half-degree error in setting the autopilot, a half-degree error in taking the bearing of Juan Point.

· · · · · · · · · · · ·

9   Canadian Hydrographic Service, *Sailing Directions: Inner Passage, Queen Charlotte Sound to Chatham Sound,* 1st ed. (2002), corrected from Notices to Mariners Monthly Edition No. 09/2015 (Ottawa: Minister of Fisheries and Oceans Canada, 2012), 2-17–2-21.

It is for these reasons that monitoring position is so important in this kind of navigation. Lilgert possibly underestimated these dangers and felt that the ship would be safe while he dealt with the problem of avoiding the traffic.

When the trees of Gil Island appeared in the cast of the ship's low-level deck lights, time and distance had pretty much run out. What little time was left burned away as the bridge crew struggled with ambiguous autopilot controls. In the time that it took Karen Briker to run to my cabin and pound on my door, they still would have been able to save the ship if they had just switched to manual steering and corrected the course with the wheel. Briker was trying to do this, but the new and complicated arrangement had her confused.[10]

It is not necessary to conclude Lilgert ignored navigation for fourteen minutes as expert witnesses claim. Nor is it requisite to assume that he was disoriented for that full period. There is no good reason to reject his testimony that he was doing exactly what he was intending to do to avoid collision with another vessel. The problem was that he did not understand how close he was getting to Gil Island because he was disoriented, or in a state of lost situational awareness. He even admitted this at his trial when he said, "I was so certain that I was three cables off [Gil Island] ... I was shocked in realizing that that wasn't where I was."[11]

Does anyone remember *getting* lost or *getting* confused? No. We remember *being* lost and we remember *not being* lost. It is the same with confusion or lost situational awareness. As a licensed commercial airplane pilot, I am familiar with an expression used in aviation to describe a certain kind of situational awareness loss: "thinking behind the airplane." It means that what the pilot thinks is taking place has already happened, and it happened behind where the airplane is now. The fact that such an expression exists reveals that the phenomenon is both recognized and understood in that industry. There are many in the marine industry with the same

· · · · · · · · · · · ·

10   James Keller, "Karl Lilgert Trial: Karen Briker Wasn't Trained On Autopilot," Canadian Press, May 3, 2013, http://www.huffingtonpost.ca/2013/03/05/karl-lilgert-trial-karen-briker-autopilot-training_n_2812881.html

11   Tyler Harbottle, "Karl Lilgert Trial: BC Ferry Officer 'Absolutely Horrified' Before Crash," Canadian Press, April 23, 2013, http://www.huffingtonpost.ca/2013/04/23/karl-lilgert-trial-bc-ferry_n_3141662.html

understanding, but, unfortunately, they seem to have been left out of the *Queen of the North* investigation and the subsequent proceedings in court.

This leads me to the question of the radar being set to the half-mile range. As I mentioned in Chapter 2, when I arrived on the bridge I found the radar set to such a short range as to render it useless for navigation in those waters. Not only was it set to the half-mile range, but the picture was also offset. The "default" setting for a radar puts the ship in the centre of the screen. With a modern radar, the position of the ship can be set anywhere on the screen (except the extreme periphery). Lilgert testified that he was experiencing a lot of trouble trying to get a clear radar picture.[12] The unusual setting of the radar supports the idea of an operator actively working at his navigation aids rather than one neglecting his duty. While Lilgert was occupied with the radar, he apparently remained confident in his geographical navigation and was unaware that he was getting too close to Gil Island. It is easy to criticize his actions with 20/20 hindsight, but I do not see any proof that he was negligent. There are so many ways to go wrong navigating the confined waters of the Inside Passage, it is seldom necessary to posit gross dereliction of duty as the explanation for an accident.[13] Slight miscalculation is often a fully adequate reason.

If it sounds like I'm defending everything Lilgert did, I'm not. He himself admits he was at fault. I think he failed in serious ways. But this speaks to proficiency, not criminality.

And I am not trying to place undue blame for the sinking on the equipment and bridge layout. I am just pointing out that if they had been better, the ship might have survived, despite human error.

It is possible, though not very likely, in my opinion, that Karl Lilgert uncharacteristically abandoned his duty and dishonoured his long record of responsible service, and that is why the *Queen of the North* was lost. But it is not correct to conclude that Karl Lilgert *must* have abandoned his duty because that is the only possible explanation for what happened. To settle on that conclusion does not serve the interests of justice or safe navigation. On the contrary, it may prevent us from learning the real lessons this disaster has to teach us.

· · · · · · · · · · · ·

12 Ibid.
13 Funk, "Karl Lilgert Trial: Safety Checks Missed by Crew, Says Mariner."

CHAPTER 7

THE AUTOMATIC PILOT

DURING THE REFIT THAT PRECEDED THE ACCIDENT, A MODIFICA-
tion was made to the ship's steering system that I believe may have contributed to the grounding. The *Queen of the North* already had a complex
and less than satisfactory steering arrangement. This dated back to when
it was built and had become progressively more complex over the years as
modifications were made.

In a small boat, all that is needed to control the rudder is a stick fastened to the top of it. Called a "tiller," this form of control remains in boat-
ing use to this day and has seen service in some fairly large craft. As ships
became larger, it was necessary to develop more sophisticated systems—
the simpler ones employed cables, pulleys, chains, and rods, but these also
had their limitations pertaining to size, so hydraulic and electrical control
systems were developed.

In the *Queen of the North*, the rudders were turned by hydraulic motors.
The impulse to control these hydraulic motors came from the bridge and
was electrical. The original steering wheel, shaped like the yoke of some
World War II bomber, was effectively an electrical switch or, rather, a series
of electrical switches. With the yoke centred, the switch was "off." When
turned to port, the switch was closed, and the rudders would rotate to
port. They would continue to rotate until the wheel was centred again, at
which point they would remain at their turned position. To bring them
back to midships (or neutral), the wheel had to be turned to starboard
and held there until the rudders reached the desired position. Essential to
this operation was the rudder angle indicator. Without that, the helmsman

could have no idea what the position of the rudders was and would be unable to steer. Steering the *Queen of the North* was an art at which not all seamen excelled.

Original equipment also included an automatic pilot. This device does not actually *pilot* the ship (as its name implies); it simply steers, keeping the ship on a selected heading (or course). The ship's original automatic pilot shared its home with the gyro compass, which looked as if it could be a distant evolutionary ancestor of R2D2. Painted in that old grey-black speckled enamel, the autopilot stood on the centre-line, at the forward bulkhead of the bridge.

Outside the wheelhouse, on each bridge wing, was a large workbench (called a "console" by some). On each of these benches was a set of instruments and propulsion controls to be used when bringing the ship alongside or when docking stern-first. Each bench also had a small lever, sometimes called a "tiller" or "jog steering." The master had the option of steering the ship with it when operating from the bridge wing.

So that provided, at four different locations, four options for steering the ship: a wheel, an autopilot, and two jog levers. Only one mode could be in use at one time. To choose the mode, one four-position rotary selector switch was located directly forward of the wheel. It was somewhat complex but logical.

The setup got a little more complicated as aging equipment had to be replaced. The first piece to go was the autopilot. It had become unreliable, so the company purchased a new one, which was much fancier than the original and came with additional features.

It still occupied the same location with roughly the same size footprint. Like the old one, its cabinet housed the master gyro compass, which fed multiple remote displays called repeaters. These were conveniently located for the various purposes of steering and taking bearings both visually and by radar. One such repeater was directly forward of the steering wheel. Another was on top of the autopilot cabinet. On the old unit, a very simple dial was fitted, superimposed on the repeater, and that is how the courses were set and adjusted.

Following the modern trend, the designers added digital displays to the new unit. The familiar analogue-display compass card upheld tradition and was still prominent, but its use was limited to displaying information. Course setting and course adjustment were performed with a stand-alone dial and its digital display. This is where things got complicated and, for some, confusing.

The old system was simplicity itself. The superimposed dial would be turned to the desired course, and then the selector switch would be set to "autopilot." Simple. Course adjustments were made by turning the dial. Skilled helmsmen learned to turn the dial at a steady pace during large course alterations in order to control the rate of turn.

The new set-up took this nice integrated system and split it into three parts. The analogue compass remained, as I have said, but a stand-alone dial was provided for the course settings. The dial, somewhat like the one you will find on a typical washing machine, could simply be turned, or it could be held down and turned. Each method provided a different mode of operation. If the dial was pushed down and turned, it operated like the old system and the course would change as the dial was being turned. Rate of turn could be controlled depending on how fast you turned the dial. If you turned the dial without pushing it down, nothing would happen except the digital readout next to the dial would change to indicate what the newly selected heading was going to be. (For those who prefer push buttons, the design nerds had provided a set of buttons with "up" and "down" arrows that did the same thing.) When the display showed the desired course, the helmsman would push a button marked "Set," and the autopilot would take this as the new course. It would then realize that it was now off course and would respond appropriately. If the alteration was large, its response would be urgent—that is, the autopilot would "think" that it was *way* off course and would apply an amount of rudder appropriate to what must surely be a big emergency. An alarm would sound, the ship would heel over and come swinging wildly around to the new course, the autopilot would sound another alarm, apply a huge amount of counter-rudder to stop the ship from overshooting the new heading, and thus cause another careening until the autopilot brought itself and the ship under control—but not before it sounded at least one more alarm. What a technological breakthrough: a panicking automaton! The most badly executed and unseamanlike turns I have ever witnessed were performed by this stupid machine. No competent seaman would ever steer like that.

Worse, the system introduced a new opportunity for error. Someone could dial in the new course but forget to push "Set," thereby leaving the ship merrily steaming along on the wrong course. This might well have been what happened the night of the sinking and would explain Lilgert's testimony that he thought the course change had been made when it hadn't.

The new dial that required two steps to set a new course was the first complication. Now we move on to the second.

The old system did have a drawback in that a changeover from auto-pilot to manual steering required the helmsman to travel some fifteen steps around an obstacle to get back to the steering wheel. This meant an emergency turn could not be carried out as quickly as would be ideal.

The new system changed that by incorporating a steering wheel in the same cabinet that housed the autopilot. Not just a steering wheel but the choice of a steering wheel or a "tiller" (jog). This, of course, necessitated another switch added to the system, one that sat on the autopilot cabinet and had three positions: "Autopilot," "Wheel," and "Tiller," each marked by a pictograph. So from four steering options at four different locations, the bridge now contained, at the same four locations, six steering options: two wheels, three jog steering levers, and the autopilot.

Although there were some non-consequential incidents caused by the difficulties some crew members had in trying to understand this system, no accidents were caused by it. Note that I do not say "*fortunately* no accidents were caused." This is because I believe that the occurrence of accidents is still necessary to safety. Without accidents, responses to unsafe situations are slow to come, if not completely absent. Had some small accident occurred and the steering system been identified as a contributing cause, the situation might have been improved and the sinking might have been prevented.

So how could this system be made worse? The original system and the new system were designed to steer by the gyro compass. But what if the gyro compass failed? In that case you simply didn't use the autopilot. You steered by hand until you reached port. When you reached port, you got the gyro fixed. It's against the law to leave port without a functioning gyro.

Some gyro failures were caused by a loss of electrical power and some were caused by the fact that some fathead put the "On/Off" switch at knee height in the very place where normal human beings were likely to put their knee (in the dark, don't forget). And, of course, the fathead placed no guard over it. In spite of these tribulations, operating without a gyro was a very rare occurrence, but someone thought we needed more paraphernalia, so they fitted yet another new module.

This new module enabled the autopilot to operate in conjunction with the magnetic compass as well as the gyro compass. A transducer was fitted to the bottom of the magnetic compass card to transmit the magnetic information to the new module in the autopilot cabinet, which converted the magnetic information to digital information.[1] Another LED was fitted to give a digital display of the magnetic information, and four more push buttons were added in order to cope with the vagaries of the magnetic compass. The autopilot unit now had a total of twenty-six push buttons, where before we had four dials of the sort that would never be activated accidentally.

As with the case of the unprotected "On/Off" gyro switch, the crew again had to improvise protective devices to try to negate the effect of all these buttons and readouts. The digital readout for the magnetic compass was covered with black tape so that it would not be confused with the visually identical and unidentified digital readouts for the gyro compass and the course selected. Hinged pieces of Plexiglas were added to cover up nine of the superfluous push buttons.

The first anomaly we noted was that the analogue gyro-compass card was lagging when the ship turned, and it frequently needed realigning. When we looked at it more closely, we discovered that it was behaving like a magnetic compass, leading or lagging in the turns. It took much longer to work out that the analogue compass card was no longer "slaved" to the gyro but to the magnetic compass. And, of course, another opportunity for error was introduced: the autopilot could be accidentally, and unwittingly, set to the magnetic rather than the true heading—a difference of more than 20 degrees on the BC coast.

At least you could always shut off the autopilot and steer by hand, right? Yes, but that was about to change.

During the summer of 2005, while sailing north from Bella Bella, the ship suffered a steering failure. The bridge crew at the time reported seeing a bright flash from the deckhead-mounted rudder angle indicator, and then both it and the bench-mounted rudder angle indicator froze,

. . . .

1   Some referred to this as a "flux-gate compass," but that is incorrect. A flux-gate compass does not contain a magnet, as a magnetic compass does. It uses a "flux valve," in which the earth's magnetic lines of force, or flux, induce a voltage in the coils. The voltage varies with the changes in the ship's heading and so can be converted to directional information.

indicating that the rudders were hard over. As I explained earlier, it was not possible to steer this ship without an indicator to tell you the rudder angle. When the failure occurred, the crew stopped the ship, an engineer was sent to the steering compartment, and, after much ado, power was restored, the systems were tested, and the ship carried on—with caution. The bad news was that no proper explanation for the failure ever surfaced. The good news was that the company sent a team of investigators who discovered this very old equipment was in the advanced stages of wear. The summer schedule was completed without further incident, and in the fall the ship went into refit. During the refit, a number of essential items in the steering system were replaced, including the main steering wheel and the rotary steering mode selector switch.

Whoever made these changes also chose to change the way both these systems operated. I have already described how the old steering wheel worked. The new wheel operated in an intuitive manner: when the wheel was amidships, the rudders were amidships. When the wheel was turned, the rudders turned correspondingly. The wheel itself became a rudder angle indicator, and there was an adjacent scale, illuminated clearly for night use. The one complaint was that when the wheel was released from the hand, it sprang back to the midships position. When it was required to hold a set amount of rudder—as when steaming in a crosswind—the helmsman had to hold the wheel in the desired position the entire time, sometimes for hours. This was a bit of a nuisance but still logical.

Not logical was the modification made to the steering mode selector switch. There were now *two* mode selector switches. One at the "after" (main) steering position and one at the "forward" unit.

In the original configuration, the forward switch was subordinate to the after switch and was only functional when the after switch was set to the position marked for the forward unit. When the after switch was set to any other position, the forward switch had no effect.

The modification changed all that. Although the switches looked the same as they had before and were marked in the same manner, their functionality had been changed significantly. With the new set-up, the autopilot could be engaged by setting the switch on the forward stand to "Auto Pilot." However, the manual steering at the forward stand could not be used unless the switch at the *aft* steering stand was set to "Fore Bridge." If it became necessary to make an emergency turn when the ship was on autopilot, the officer of the watch had to know which procedure had been followed when going *on* to autopilot. This would determine exactly what switch or switches he had to select in order to regain manual control of the steering, and which of the steering wheels (don't forget that this bridge now has *two* steering wheels) he would be getting the use of. If he was uncertain, he would have to troubleshoot.[2]

The two groups of switches were separated by distance and by the obstacle of the aft steering stand. This meant the two groups of switches could not be read or operated by one person standing in one place. Furthermore, the engine controls were situated approximately 10 feet (3 metres) away from both of these groups of switches. As I have said, all this was inconvenient at the best of times, a nightmare on March 22, 2006.

The TSB Report noted that "various B watch deck crew provided investigators with four different explanations as to the interaction between the forward and aft steering station switches and which specific functions were available at various switch settings," and claimed that this demonstrated the crew's unfamiliarity with the new equipment.[3] Unfortunately, the report does not indicate what positions these various deck crew held, whether any of the four mates (whose exclusive job it was to operate these switches) were among them, or whether any of the four mates had it wrong. Given the fact that all four mates had been using the autopilot without difficulty throughout the week preceding the accident, it seems unlikely they did not understand it. However, there is a difference between operating new equipment in the clear light of day, when one has all the time and room in the world, and operating it in the dark when one is under the pressure of imminent disaster.

The indications for the steering switches in the *Queen of the North* should have been clear, logical, and unambiguous. The active switch and switching pathway should have been laid out and backlit in such a way that its selected mode was apparent at a glance. A graphical layout of the switches or, at least, a self-explanatory block diagram should have been provided in such a way as to eliminate all mystery. Such systems are used almost exclusively in aircraft for critical systems like fuel tank and cross-feed selection.

The situation with the *Queen of the North* was comparable to that of the offshore oil platform *Ocean Ranger* on February 15, 1982. In the *Ocean*

. . . .

2   TSB Report, 19–21, 39, 49.

3   TSB Report, 20.

Ranger's case, the ballast operator was misled by the layout and labelling of the ballast control system. Believing that he was pumping water out of the low side, he pumped water in. The *Ocean Ranger* sank. Eighty-four people died.

In her paper "Human Error and Marine Safety," Dr. Anita M. Rothblum of the US Coast Guard Research and Development Center examined the case of the oil tanker *Torrey Canyon*, which ran aground on Pollard Rock on the Seven Stones Reef, near Land's End, Cornwall:

> The final human error was an equipment design error (made by the equipment manufacturer). The steering selector switch was in the wrong position: it had been left on autopilot.
>
> Unfortunately, the design of the steering selector unit did not give any indication of its setting at the helm. So when the captain ordered a turn into the western channel through the Scillies the helmsman dutifully turned the wheel, but nothing happened. By the time they figured out the problem and got the steering selector back on "manual", it was too late to make the turn, and the TORREY CANYON ran aground.
>
> As these ... examples show, there are many different kinds of human error. It is important to recognize that "human error" encompasses much more than what is commonly called "operator error". In order to understand what causes human error, we need to consider how humans work within the maritime system.[4]

Like Rothblum, I believe "'human error' encompasses much more than what is commonly called 'operator error.'" I believe it is also human error to design, produce, purchase, and install sub-standard equipment.

The situation on the bridge of the *Queen of the North* was even worse than the one on the *Torrey Canyon*; it was necessary to visit both stations and examine the respective settings and then interpret them correctly in order to understand the status of the steering system.

. . . .

4   The paper is available online at the National Energy Board website, https://docs .neb-one.gc.ca/ll-eng/llisapi.dll/Open/2786106

In its report on a hard landing by BC Ferries' *Coastal Inspiration* in 2011, TSB made this observation: "For crew to be able to respond efficiently and effectively to emergency situations, it is imperative that they be able to recognize the status of all systems used in the operation of the vessel and react in a timely manner when a system fails."[5] The observation should also have been applied to the *Queen of the North* and the difficulty encountered by the bridge crew when trying to switch to manual steering in time to avoid the accident. Karen Briker testified that she did not know where the switch was (Divisional Inquiry)[6] or how to operate it (trial).[7] The Divisional Inquiry claimed that "as the autopilot disengages simply with a single switch ... and would have been operated numerous times by the QM, this testimony is difficult to reconcile,"[8] but in fact the autopilot engaged and disengaged according to various combinations of *two* multiple-position switches located several feet apart. Briker would not have operated these switches numerous times, as this was one of her first times on the ship since the refit; she might never have operated them at all, as this was the OOW's responsibility. The TSB Report noted that "in the original system and the B watch system, the QM would normally only be required to operate the steering-mode selector switch at the aft steering station," but she was at the forward station.[9] And at trial, Briker testified that she was not trained to operate the switch because "procedures in place at the time saw the quartermaster at the wheel while the officer on the bridge changed the autopilot setting, ensuring there would be someone on the wheel when it was switched to manual steering."[10]

TSB came close to hitting the nail on the head with the statement "BC

· · · · · · · · · · · ·

5   Transportation Safety Board, "Striking of Berth: Roll-on/Roll-off Ferry *Coastal Inspiration*, Duke Point, British Columbia, 20 December 2011," Marine Investigation Report M11W0211 (http://www.tsb.gc.ca/eng/rapports-reports/marine/2011/m11w0211 /m11w0211.asp), 13.

6   Divisional Inquiry, 14.

7   James Keller, "Karl Lilgert Trial: Karen Briker Wasn't Trained on Autopilot," Canadian Press, May 3, 2013, http://www.huffingtonpost.ca/2013/03/05/karl-lilgert -trial-karen-briker-autopilot-training_n_2812881.html

8   Divisional Inquiry, 14.

9   TSB Report, 21, 5.

10   Keller, "Karl Lilgert Trial: Karen Briker Wasn't Trained On Autopilot."

Ferries did not make a thorough risk/training needs analysis following changes made to the vessel's steering-mode selector switch."[11] I would suggest that the company needed to make the risk analysis *before* making the changes.

TRAINING

On the subject of training, TSB said:

> It is important that personnel skills be upgraded to keep pace with technological and operational changes. In this instance, the 4/O had received no formal ECS training and had not—despite advances in radar technology—had SEN refresher training, neither was this required by regulations.
>
> In the absence of regulatory or industry-wide standards for ensuring that officers have received up-to-date training appropriate to the equipment they use, some mariners may lack the skills required to operate modern bridge equipment.[12]

My belief is that rather than constantly training the crew for constantly changing equipment, the opposite approach is better. First, draw up appropriate standards for the equipment. This would go a long way to reduce the need for training. Next, provide the crews with any and all information that they can use. Then, *if* there remains some need for training, draw up standards *for the training.* The blind cannot lead the blind. This applies to everyone: designers, trainers, and regulators. It must be recognized that "training" in this industry runs the full range from very good to very bad, and mostly tends toward the bad. Furthermore, instructors—whether at BC Ferries or at technical institutes in British Columbia or anywhere else—are trained to varying degrees in instructional technique but carry no special qualifications in subject matter. To use TSB's language, "neither was this required by regulations," as if the title of "instructor" magically bestows specialized knowledge on the people teaching the courses.

. . . .

11   TSB Report, 49.

12   TSB Report, 50.

In aviation, instructors have the minimum of a commercial pilot licence plus whatever endorsement they might be teaching (multi-engine, instruments, seaplane, etc.) plus an Instructor rating. This rating requires not only instructional technique but also enhanced subject matter expertise. No such marine equivalent exists. Another important difference is that flight instructors are current, practising pilots; marine instructors are usually retired from seafaring. Not helping the problem is the fact that marine training centres pay lower wages than what mariners can get elsewhere, so there is difficulty attracting instructors.

When training is provided, it has to be designed to ensure the crew can operate equipment without stopping to think about what buttons to push. In May 2006, the TSB sent BC Ferries Marine Safety Advisory Letter 07/06, which stated, "Information gathered so far has revealed that some bridge team members were not familiar with the use of all of the bridge equipment and controls." The letter specifically mentioned the "recently installed steering-mode selector switch" and the various settings for the ECS display, and suggested that "BCFS may wish to take measures to ensure that, following modifications made to a vessel, crew members are fully familiarized with and trained to operate new or modified equipment such that they are prepared to be able to safely carry out their duties."[13]

In response, the BC Ferries president, David Hahn, was quoted as saying, "[I don't] understand why anyone would attempt to sail a vessel—especially a passenger ferry—if they weren't comfortable with its safety features." He said, "I would argue very strongly they should have stood up and said, 'I can't sail the ship.'"[14] But Jackie Miller, president of the Ferry Workers' Union, said that "speaking out only gets her members into trouble. 'BC Ferries has consciously made decisions in the past to sail vessels that we deem, and our members deem, to be unsafe, and if

. . . .

13   Letter available at the CBC website, www.cbc.ca/bc/news/060606_tsb-letter.pdf

14   Dirk Meissner, "B.C. Ferry Boss Frustrated That Safety Concerns Surfaced after Deadly Sinking," Canadian Press, June 6, 2006. In the same article, Hahn appeared to downplay the changes in the equipment: "An autopilot existed on this ship before the new one was put in. It's not like they've never used an autopilot before." But this was part of the problem. The new autopilot was just different enough from the old one that it risked causing confusion in a crisis.

expressions of concern are raised the crew members, the ships' officers, are disciplined for it.'"[15]

After receiving the TSB's Marine Safety Advisory Letter, BC Ferries set in place a new procedure "requiring all officers to sign documents affirming they are completely comfortable with the operation of any modified or newly installed equipment. 'We do the same training,' Hahn said, 'but we're asking the officers now to actually sign a piece of paper that they actually are now fully acquainted with the operation of the equipment.'"[16] However, I'm certain that all four officers on "B" crew the night the *Queen of the North* sank were sure they were "fully acquainted with the operation of the equipment" and would have signed the piece of paper. A signature on a piece of paper does not mean that operation has become second nature when they suddenly realize they are not where they think they are and they have only seconds to push the right buttons in the right sequence to avoid disaster.

PILOT TRAPS

And while I agree with the principle of training, no amount of training or understanding of the ECS, for example, or the radar would have made up for their deficiencies. The situation would have remained the same. TSB wrote that "BC Ferries crew members were not fully familiarized with new safety-critical equipment installed during refit,"[17] but my view is that the equipment was so bad, no amount of familiarization would make up for it. Aeronautical engineers refer to such bad ergonomics as "pilot traps." TSB referred to "advances in radar technology." In my opinion there have been some backward steps taken in newer, not necessarily better, radar technology. The move to digital radar screens was mostly the result of cost saving and had nothing to do with providing a better radar picture. In fact, I believe the move to digital made the radars less convenient to use.

For example, the quick and easy task of setting a parallel index line was turned into a long, counter-intuitive process involving drop-down menus

· · · · · · · · · · · ·

15 "Union Levels Broadside at BC Ferries Management," CBC News, June 7, 2006, http://www.cbc.ca/news/canada/union-levels-broadside-at-bc-ferries-management-1.583588

16 Ibid.

17 TSB Report, 54.

PARALLEL INDEX

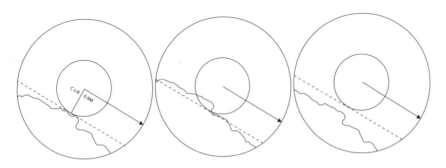

In this radar technique, a line is superimposed on the screen and made to lie parallel with the intended course. It is offset from the ship (at the centre of the screen) by the required distance from the shore or beacon. In this example, the ship's heading marker is the line with the arrowhead. The parallel index line is the dashed one. The ship is navigated by holding the parallel index against the reference mark (left), which in this case is the edge of an island. If the line appears to move toward (middle) or away from (right) the island's edge, the ship is off course.

and numerous steps. What should have taken seconds now took minutes. It also required the complete concentration of the operator throughout those minutes, to the exclusion of everything else that was going on. Once set, the parallel index line could not be adjusted except by a repetition of the entire process. Parallel indexing, the most important navigational technique in radar navigation, was rendered practically useless.

REGULATIONS IN BRIDGE DESIGN
AND STEERING CHANGEOVER

Although not in reaction to the *Queen of the North* sinking, the section of Canada's Navigation Safety Regulations concerning bridge design has improved since 2006.[18] At the time of the sinking, the regulations were very

. . . .

18   Available online at the Justice Laws website, http://laws-lois.justice.gc.ca/eng /regulations/sor-2005-134/FullText.html

weak. Still, the "Principles Relating to Bridge Design and Arrangement of Navigational Equipment and Bridge Procedures" from the Navigation Safety Regulations (in 2006) state specifically that "(13) Equipment … that offers alternative modes of operation shall indicate the actual mode of use." These principles also say that

> 6.(1) … all decisions that concern navigational equipment, navigational visibility, steering gear, equipment relating to charts and nautical publications … and that affect bridge design, the design and arrangement of navigational equipment on the bridge and bridge procedures, shall be made with the aim of (a) facilitating the tasks to be performed by the bridge team … in making a full appraisal of the situation and in navigating the ship safely under all operational conditions; … (c) enabling the bridge team … to have convenient and continuous access to essential information presented in a clear and unambiguous manner, using standardized symbols and coding systems for controls and displays; (d) indicating the operational status of automated functions and integrated components, systems and sub-systems; … (f) preventing or minimizing excessive or unnecessary work and any conditions or distractions on the bridge that could cause fatigue or interfere with the vigilance of the bridge team … ; and (g) minimizing the risk of human error.

British Columbia's Occupational Health and Safety Regulations applied to the ships just as they did to any other workplace. Article 12.10 stated clearly that "controls and switches [must be] clearly identified to indicate the functions they serve" and "must be in easy reach of the operator." Our controls and switches were anything but clearly identified or within easy reach.

The American Bureau of Shipping (ABS), in its "Guide for Bridge Design and Navigational Equipment / Systems,"[19] recommends that "displays and control devices … be arranged in a functional and logical manner to allow the operator an easy and clear means of identification of each of the

· · · · · · · · · · · ·

19 The "Guide for Bridge Design and Navigational Equipment / Systems" is available on the ABS website, http://ww2.eagle.org/en/rules-and-resources/rules-and-guides.html

components or systems" (B3.5). It further recommends, for autopilots, "an overriding control device ... at the navigation and traffic surveillance/maneuvering workstation. The override control is to enable instant take-over from the autopilot as well as from the manual steering station" (C13.2.3). The ABS Guidelines were not law, but following these recommendations would probably have prevented the grounding and subsequent sinking.

The International Maritime Organization's Marine Safety Committee put forward Resolution MSC 67 in 1996, which included the following recommendation for changing over from automatic to manual steering and vice versa:

> 4.1 Change-over from automatic to manual steering and vice-versa ... should be effected by one manual control within 3 seconds.
>
> 4.4 There should be a single change-over control which should be located in such a position that it is easily accessible to the officer of the watch.
>
> 4.5 Adequate indication should be provided to show which method of steering is in operation.[20]

In aviation, the regulations are more specific. Canadian Airworthiness Regulation 523.1329 addresses the automatic pilot system:

> (a) Each system must be designed so that the automatic pilot can (1) be quickly and positively disengaged by the pilots to prevent it from interfering with their control of the aeroplane ... (b) the quick release (emergency) control must be located on the control wheel (both control wheels if the aeroplane can be operated from either pilot seat) on the side opposite the throttles ... (d) Each manually operated control for the system must be readily accessible to the pilot.[21]

· · · · · · · · · · · ·

20   IMO Maritime Safety Committee, "Adoption of New and Amended Performance Standards," Resolution MSC.64(67), 10, http://www.imo.org/blast/blastData.asp?doc _id=6786&filename=64(67).pdf

21   The Canadian Aviation Regulations are available on the Transport Canada website, https://www.tc.gc.ca/eng/civilaviation/regserv/cars/part5-standards-523-sub-f-2064.htm

In other words, at the pilot's fingertips. As for the labels on controls, Canadian Airworthiness Regulation 525.1555 says that "Each cockpit control, other than primary flight controls and controls whose function is obvious, must be plainly marked as to its function and method of operation."

In TSB Aviation Report No. A97H0002, which involved the risk of a collision between two airliners that "occurred as the result of an ineffective controller handover procedure," the Transportation Safety Board made a relevant observation about the layout of the air traffic control tower:

> In its March 1990 special investigation report into Air Traffic Control Services in Canada, the Canadian Aviation Safety Board (CASB) concluded that "the current lack of integration of information required airport controllers to monitor several displays and information sources to make critical decisions." It was noted in one Transport Canada Fact Finding Board (FFB) report that **the controller had to move 15 feet from his work station** to visually check the ASDE [radar used to detect movement of planes and vehicles on the ground at an airport] display. In view of the inefficiencies in the layout of airport controller's information displays, the CASB recommended that "the Department of Transport accelerate the improvement of control tower layouts with a view to implementing an ergonomically efficient configuration."[22] (emphasis added)

Coincidentally, the distance between the two steering system switches in the *Queen of the North* was also 15 feet (4.6 metres).

. . . .

22 Transportation Safety Board, "Risk of Collision between Avionair Inc. Swearingen Aviation Metro II C-GBXX and Air Canada Canadair Ltd. CL-600 Regional Jet C-FSKI, Ottawa/MacDonald-Cartier International Airport, 12 March 1997," Aviation Report No. A97H0002 (http://www.tsb.gc.ca/eng/rapports-reports/aviation/1997/a97h0002 /a97h0002.asp), i, 9.

CHAPTER 8

SECOND GUESSING

ALTHOUGH THE TRANSPORTATION SAFETY BOARD EXPLORED THE wreck with a remote control submersible and went to greater lengths in its investigation of the sinking than any other agency, I personally found some of its findings puzzling. Everyone else who commented on the incident, including the BC Ferries Divisional Inquiry, singled out the safe evacuation of the crew and passengers for high praise, calling it "professional" and "heroic." When it came the turn of the TSB, however, the investigators could find little good to say. For example, rather than simply stating that an error was made when people were counted as they went into rafts and boats, the report says, "No accurate head count of passengers and crew was taken before abandoning the vessel thus precluding a focused search for missing persons at that time."[1]

In fact, every effort was made to take an accurate head count, and the ship was searched for passengers. The cabins were methodically searched using sound procedures, including the cabin that had been let to the two passengers who later turned out to be missing; they were not there. All areas accessible to passengers were searched. In the last minutes before sinking I personally made a final inspection of the passenger areas at a dead run. We could not have searched the ship more than we did because it was sinking and we had exhausted all the time available. Our own rescue

. . . .
1   TSB Report, 53.

boat plus two fishing boats searched the surrounding waters immediately before and after the sinking. In the hours following the Coast Guard, supported by a flotilla of volunteer vessels, conducted a grid search of the entire sound and shore areas in accordance with International Air and Marine Search and Rescue procedures.

When I joined BC Ferries' Northern Service in 1988, there was no formal emergency procedure for conducting cabin searches. I changed this by instituting a cabin search routine and establishing equipment for the job. This included (in both the *Queen of the North* and the *Queen of Prince Rupert*) a dedicated key cabinet with master keys for emergency use only, a dedicated cache of flashlights, and the dedicated supply of chalk to be issued to each person engaged in the searches. I wrote detailed instructions for each crew member. These were kept in a binder for reference by the crew. (An example of a crew member's cabin search duties is in Appendix D.)

When it came to comment on exercises and drills, the TSB called the drills "mundane" and "inadequate," stating that that the crew were "ill-prepared to handle some aspects of the abandonment, thereby placing passengers at risk."[2] This does not square with the fact that the crew carried out an effective and timely evacuation of the ship when the real deal struck, maintaining order and covering all the bases. During the abandonment, only one error was made—a matter of counting heads—which is more difficult on a sinking ship in the middle of the night than you might think. It did not "preclude a focused search for missing persons" because the search effort was based on the assumption people might be missing.

The TSB Report stated that "the master and the crew had to rely on their own experience to set up the drills, without the benefit or guidance of official advance planning."[3] This is correct and reflects an appeal I had made repeatedly to the corporation to implement an evacuation plan, but it also has the unfortunate effect of discrediting the very effective planning that we undertook and carried out on our own.

. . . .

2   TSB Report, 47.

3   TSB Report, 47.

WATERTIGHT DOORS

The issue of watertight doors also received a lot of attention from the TSB. Each of the eleven bulkheads on Decks 1 and 2 had one door to permit passengers and crew to pass through. The regulations governing the construction of ships specify very exactly how these doors must be built. One criterion is that they must have controls located on both sides of the door as well as two more sets of remote controls for emergency use: one on the bridge and one at another remote location. An additional criterion is that the doors must be located near the centre-line of the ship so that they are protected in the event of a collision.

The TSB Report faulted the operator for not having all watertight doors shut at the time of grounding, on the premise that running with all doors shut is simply a given:

> By not ensuring that the integrity of subdivision measures, such as watertight bulkheads and doors, was maintained at all times while the vessel was in operation, the potential to slow down or stem the progressive flooding of the vessel was not realized. Any delay in ensuring that all watertight doors are closed can contribute to progressive flooding into compartments other than those initially damaged.[4]

There are two conflicting schools of thought concerning watertight doors. One view holds that every watertight door must be kept closed when the ship is at sea except for occasional and momentary openings when it is necessary for someone to pass through for the "safe working of the ship." I don't know what other kind of "working of the ship" there would be, and this imprecise wording only clouds the issue. Those who believe the doors should be kept closed argue that, in the event of flooding, it might not be possible to close a door that is open at the time of a collision or grounding. They speculate that the door or its mechanism could be damaged, or a loose item could fall or float into the opening and prevent the door from closing.

. . . .

4   TSB Report, 41.

The opposing view points out that the doors are there for a reason: people, especially engineers, must pass through them regularly in the course of their duties. Engineers are moving through the doors all the time, often carrying tools or parts, and doing so in every kind of sea condition from smooth to very rough. Many, if not most, of the people on board hold the view that the overall safety of the ship and its crew and passengers would favour leaving the doors in the open position. The Safety of Life at Sea (SOLAS) Convention supports this view: "Certain watertight doors may be permitted to remain open during navigation only if considered absolutely necessary; that is, being open is determined to be essential to the safe and effective operation of the ship's machinery or to permit passengers normally unrestricted access throughout the passenger area. Such determination shall be made by the Administration [respective government] only after careful consideration of the impact on ship operations and survivability" (SOLAS Chapter II-1, Regulation 15, Article 9.3).

By leaving the determination up to the respective governments, SOLAS recognizes the fact that the designs of some ships are simply not suited to a policy of keeping the doors closed. The *Queen of the North*, with its complex machinery spaces and below-deck accommodations for both passengers and crew, fell into just such a classification. And uppermost in the minds of those who crewed the ship was the memory of the Second Engineer in the *Queen of Prince Rupert*, who was crushed to death when attempting to pass through a watertight door.

The opposing factions did not belong to any one body. Some people in BC Ferries, Transport Canada, and the nautical profession generally, believed watertight doors should be kept open; others believed they should be kept closed. Transport Canada had ruled that it would be acceptable for the *Queen of the North* to run with the doors open, and this was reflected in company policy. However, the dissenters would not be silenced. Eventually, a compromise was reached. The *Queen of the North* and the *Queen of Prince Rupert* would sail with all but two watertight doors closed, an important fact to remember. The two doors that would remain open were on either side of the main engine room: one leading to the workshop; the other leading to the generator (or auxiliary engine) room. (BC Ferries, in its Divisional Inquiry, notes: "At sea it was normal practice on the vessel that all watertight doors were closed except two in the engine room spaces which were open for the safe working of the engine room."[5])

As part of the compromise, passengers were no longer allowed below the car deck. This caused considerable loss of revenue, as there were passenger cabins on Deck 2. Crew, however, continued to be accommodated below the car deck.

TRANSPORTATION SAFETY BOARD EXPLANATION OF THE GROUNDING

Contrary to the statement in the *Canadian Transportation Accident Investigation and Safety Board Act* that "no finding of the [TSB] shall be construed as assigning fault or determining civil or criminal liability" (section 7(3)), all the proceedings that followed the TSB inquiry into the sinking of the *Queen of the North*, including the criminal trial of the Fourth Mate, drew heavily on the board's findings. So what did the TSB Report say about what happened on March 22, 2006?

In the absence of a voyage data recorder (VDR), the TSB had difficulty in arriving at a conclusive explanation. The closest Marine Investigation Report M06W0052 into the sinking of the *Queen of the North* comes to an explanation is this:

2.1.1 MISSED COURSE CHANGE

When undertaking routine tasks, it is possible for a distraction to cause a sequential step to be missed and for persons in such circumstances to believe that the missed step and those that follow have in fact been accomplished.

In this instance, between the time the 4/O [fourth officer] announced to MCTS that the vessel was approaching Sainty Point and the time the course change should have been made (3.5 minutes), the OOW's [officer of the watch—in other words, Karl Lilgert's] routine sequence

. . . .
5   Divisional Inquiry, 25.

of making a course change was interrupted by several events that were taking place simultaneously, including:

- the 4/O and QM1 [quartermaster, Karen Briker] were engaged in a conversation of a personal nature;
- the vessel was encountering a rapidly moving squall, causing reduced visibility; and
- a visual alarm indicating a loss of target.

In dealing with the immediate requirement to identify the position of the lost target, combined with the effects of entering the squall, the 4/O was likely distracted at some point between logging the radio communication and carrying out the course change. As a result, he believed he had called for and verified the course alteration.[6]

Several assumptions are made here. For one, there is nothing that compels the navigator to alter course when the ship is abeam Sainty Point. The navigator has a number of options and a great deal of freedom as to when and where to alter course—it may be altered before reaching Sainty Point or may safely be altered well after passing it. In fact, Lilgert testified that he did not miss the course change: he delayed it.

The second point to note is that the report is not actually saying that Lilgert was distracted, only that there were events which *might* have been distracting. In my opinion, the report goes a little too far in the matter-of-fact way in which it states what is only speculation: "the 4/O was likely distracted ... As a result, he believed he had called for and verified the course alteration." When reading any TSB investigation report, it is important to bear in mind that TSB bases its findings on such things as personal testimonies, records, and physical evidence. The sources of the testimonies are unnamed in the report, and they are not usually quoted verbatim, making it difficult to determine just how much inference and deduction goes into the findings.

The report goes on to say:

. . . .

6   TSB Report, 37.

> The TSB examined a number of plausible scenarios. In
> the absence of objective data, such as from a VDR, the
> investigation was unable to explain why the 4/O and QM1
> did not follow basic watchkeeping practices so as to keep
> the vessel on course—nor why the 4/O failed to detect
> the vessel's improper course for up to 14 minutes.[7]

The report does not discuss these "plausible scenarios" or even state what they were. The most obvious "plausible scenario" is the one given by the only person in a position to know, Karl Lilgert, who said he chose to delay the course alteration in order to avoid collision with another vessel. The assertion that the course was improper for a full fourteen minutes is based on the assumption that Lilgert simply forgot to alter course at Sainty Point and thereafter failed to monitor the vessel's progress and so sailed blindly into Gil Island. Since Lilgert testified that he planned to clear Gil Island by 3 cables and set his course accordingly, it must be said that the course he followed was appropriate to the circumstances as he understood them. Only for the last few minutes before the grounding could the ship's course be said to be "improper" in that the ship was closing on Gil Island by less than the planned 3 cables, although it could still have been corrected safely if Lilgert had been aware of his position. There is no doubt that he failed over these last few minutes to determine his position or his course made good, but no one has been able to determine exactly why there was such a failure, and this is the one essential thing that needs to be determined. The fact that he did not realize his position until two minutes before grounding does not lead inescapably to the conclusion he was having sex, arguing, smoking marijuana, discussing real estate, or was otherwise "distracted." He might have been too absorbed in trying to make the less-than-ideal new radar perform to remember to verify the course adjustment he says he had by now called for or to use the radar to keep track of position. Any one of a number of equipment failures, such as the random fault in the electrical steering that was reported in 2005 or the tricky new autopilot control, might have confounded him. As mentioned in the previous chapter, he or the quartermaster might have dialled the new course into the autopilot but forgotten to push "Set." Any of these

. . . .

7   TSB Report, 38.

"plausible scenarios" might well lead to a finding that Lilgert had erred despite making his best effort rather than because he was distracted.

Many critics assumed that he must have been distracted simply because he was sharing the bridge with a former lover. But just how plausible is this hypothesis, really? As mentioned earlier, the bridge of a moving ship is a poor place for any kind of intimate encounter. Both supposed culprits were mature adults, not adolescents subject to losing their heads in a rush of hormones. And truth be told, romantic interactions are not so rare among BC Ferries employees. Marriages within the company are common, as are breakups and affairs, as in many large organizations. Nobody in this day and age should be shocked to hear this. Nor is it justifiable to conclude that two people can't behave professionally on the job just because they had an off-duty relationship. If that were the case, there would be many more ships grounding.

Meanwhile, Lilgert seemed alert and undistracted at 12:03 AM when he made his Sainty Point call-in to Rupert Traffic and gave an ETA for the next calling-in point at Kingcome Point. To do this he would have had to plan his next several course alterations and calculate the ship's travel time, which indicates the navigational moves necessary to transit Wright Sound were clear in his mind. To propose that this apparently competent mental state was suddenly overcome by personal issues during the next fourteen minutes of high-stress navigation is itself a highly implausible scenario that calls for a more likely explanation of events.

THE ELECTRONIC CHART SYSTEM (ECS)

Much has been made of the contention that the ship's ECS and several navigational alarms connected to the system were not being used to their full potential. First it must be understood that running with many of the navigational alarms disabled was common practice on the ship and not just Lilgert's personal choice. There were reasons for this. Proponents of ECS speak highly of the impressive potential of electronic charts but overlook the massive flaws that rendered the ECS on the *Queen of the North* almost unusable. It was never the primary navigation system and never could be.

The TSB Report summarized the features of an electronic chart system:

> ECS is a navigation information system that electronically displays vessel position and relevant nautical chart data. It

provides chart information with real-time vessel position and navigation information. It also provides alerts and prompts for track monitoring, planned course alterations, and other navigation and safety features, including continuous data recording for later analysis. These include waypoint alarms, which sound once a desired waypoint is reached and a course alteration is required, and cross-track error (XTE) alarms, which are activated when the vessel leaves the course line's set parameters. When vector charts are used, a navigation-danger alarm may be set up that establishes a radius of navigation danger centered on the ship's position. The area delineated within this circle is then constantly checked for any dangers pre-determined by the user.[8]

The equipment fitted in the *Queen of the North* could never achieve a practical application of any of these potential features for the following reasons:

- The symbol indicating the ship's position on the chart was so faint as to be practically unreadable. We could not spend the time and attention required to locate it under any but the least urgent of conditions.
- The computer software used to program this equipment was best described as "user hostile." Only the crudest and most haphazard form of passage planning was available, it required a huge amount of time and concentrated attention, and it could be altered without the navigator's knowledge or erased completely without his authorization. (My standing orders stipulated that no reliance was to be placed on any line found on any electronic chart.)
- The procedures imagined by the designers conflicted with the best navigational practices.
- The Inside Passage taken by the *Queen of North* required her to be as close as a tenth of a mile (0.19 kilometres) offshore a great deal of the time and closer still in certain parts, which made the notion of a "radius of navigation danger centred on the ship's position" impracticable.

· · · · · · · · · · · ·

8   TSB Report, 16–17.

The TSB Report stated,

> The setup of the navigational equipment hampered effective monitoring, including:
>
> - The brightness on the ECS monitor had been turned down such that the display could not be read.
> - The ECS cross-track alarm, which would have alerted the crew to any substantial deviation, was turned off.
> - The navigation-danger alarm on the ECS, which could have indicated the close proximity of Gil Island, was unavailable because a raster chart was loaded.
> - Alarms available with other electronic equipment (for example, radars) were not set up or enabled.[9]

In my view, it was not so much the set-up of the equipment but the equipment itself that hampered effective monitoring. In the first place, the nature of the ECS on the *Queen of the North* made it impractical for the navigator to lay out his own intended track, keep it secure, and call it up for his own use.

Secondly, deviating from a planned track is often a practical and even necessary option. If Lilgert, in this case, deviated in order to avoid a collision—which is entirely plausible—the "off-track alarm," if enabled, would have sounded and subsequently been silenced by Lilgert. It would not have drawn his attention to anything he did not already know about and it would have been a distraction, something his critics agreed was unhelpful. Designers of electronic navigational instruments have for many years been coming up with all kinds of alarms, but it is extremely rare for any of these to be practical. A full understanding of navigation is required before there could be any hope of such a thing.

The TSB finding that "The navigation-danger alarm on the ECS ... was unavailable because a raster chart was loaded" is a statement of fact. The raster was the only type of electronic chart in existence for much of that area of the BC coast in 2006, which is why it was loaded, even though it did not provide a navigation-danger alarm.

· · · · · · · · · · · ·

9   TSB Report, 38.

One safety feature that would have been useful had it been fitted is the chronometric gyro compass repeater, so named because of the way the instrument clicks in steps (in the manner of a chronometer) as the dial rotates. The clicks are audible and will betray any unwanted turning or, conversely, failure to turn. This type of device has prevented many a disaster. The decision to fit a silent type of gyro repeater in the *Queen of the North* was made by BC Ferries without input from me.

BASIC PRINCIPLES OF SAFE NAVIGATION

The TSB continues with this statement: "As well, a number of basic principles of safe navigation were not observed by the bridge team."[10] The report criticized Lilgert for not calling the senior officer of the watch or the master to the bridge when visibility became reduced and the location of the radar target was lost; not maintaining an effective lookout; not posting a dedicated lookout during a time of restricted visibility; not communicating with the target vessel; and not monitoring the vessel's progress visually, via radar, and with the ECS.

Dealing with this last issue first, in Chapter 6 I discussed the fact that one of the radars was set to a very short range, with the display offset to the western section. This suggests to me that the Fourth Mate was confused about how to a handle a difficult situation and may have been having trouble with the equipment, but not that he was "abandoning his duty."

There have been great improvements in navigation equipment in recent years, but not every change has been an improvement. The TSB Report refers to a "lost target," the image of a smaller vessel that came to be lost in the clutter—unwanted echoes from waves and precipitation—displayed on the radar screen. With the best analogue radars, a good radar observer can still distinguish targets through the clutter. With poorer radars, particularly digital ones, this is not possible.

The other criticisms listed above also suggest to me that the real problem was in the Fourth Mate's assessment of his situation. There is no reason to think that the bridge team was not keeping a lookout to the best of its abilities, given the conditions it was operating under. We do know that

· · · · · · · · · · · ·

10   TSB Report, 38.

the quartermaster sighted the island the moment it became visible. There would have been nothing wrong with posting an additional lookout or calling the Second Mate and/or the master, but the real problem was with the Fourth Mate's assessment of his situation. All evidence points to the fact he did not perceive how close to the island he was.

Communicating or, more likely, *attempting* to communicate with the unknown target vessel might have proved profitable, but based on my decades of experience, I can testify that such a course of action rarely produces a satisfactory result, and usually produces no result at all. Therefore, it is almost always a waste of time in a situation where time is of the essence. Not only is it a waste of time, but the layout of equipment, placed all over the *Queen of the North's* bridge, meant the Fourth Mate would have had to leave his radar—which, even with the clutter, was his first line of defence against collision—in order to reach his radio.

The report also noted another "basic principle of safe navigation" it felt the Fourth Mate did not observe was locating and identifying the navigational lights at Point Cumming, Cape Farewell, and Sainty Point. Given that the report faults the Fourth Mate for not taking appropriate action to deal with the restricted visibility prevailing at the time, is it consistent to fault him for failing to identify lights that would likely have been obscured by the same conditions? Cape Farewell would have been between 2 and 3 miles (3.7 and 5.6 kilometres) away during this period, and Point Cumming between 4 and 8 miles (7.4 and 14.8 kilometres), both too distant to be seen in thick weather.

One basic principle of safe navigation noted by the TSB that Lilgert may not have observed was verifying the course after Sainty Point. He may have ordered the course change, as he testified, but did not verify that it was carried out properly by the quartermaster (a verification that was even more crucial because this particular quartermaster was less familiar with the new, confusing equipment). Two final principles the TSB said were not observed were reducing the speed when the vessel encountered an area of reduced visibility, and maintaining an appropriate bridge team composition. Given that Lilgert apparently did not know precisely where his ship was, it is perfectly acceptable to say that the ship was travelling too fast. Any speed would have been too much. Similarly, losing sight—both by eye and by radar—of the other vessel is a cue to bring the speed right down to the minimum at which it could be kept on course. But, as I have said, the real problem appears to have been that Lilgert thought he *did* know where he was.

NAVIGATIONAL WATCH

In its report, the TSB refers to the Crewing Regulations and contends:

> The language of the *Crewing Regulations* has led to differing interpretations. Nonetheless, a plain language reading leads to the conclusion that the minimum bridge watch required by the *Crewing Regulations* in the context of the *Queen of the North* at the time of the occurrence was intended to be as follows:
>
> - a qualified person in charge of the watch (the OOW); and
> - an additional person who holds one of an efficient deck hand certificate, an able seaman certificate, or a bridge watchman certificate.
>
> Whenever the use of the automatic steering system was not appropriate—for example, when prompt helm action might be required due to encountering situations such as restricted visibility—then a second additional person was required. Under these circumstances, only one of either the additional person or the second additional person must hold one of the aforementioned certificates. The other does not, provided that he or she is assigned to the deck watch as a rating under training for the purpose of obtaining a certificate.[11]

I agree that the regulations are difficult to read and understand. They

· · · · · · · · · · · ·

11   TSB Report, 40–41. The Crewing Regulations (SOR 97-390) were in force between April 11, 2002, and July 1, 2007, when they were superseded by the Marine Personnel Regulations (SOR 2007-115). Readers are cautioned that the Crewing Regulations of 2002, not the Marine Personnel Regulations, should be referred to when examining the case of the sinking of the *Queen of the North*. They are available online at https://www.canlii .org/en/ca/laws/regu/sor-97-390/latest/sor-97-390.html

require the closest examination to reach an accurate understanding of what they require. The first and most important issue is that the regulations do not stipulate anywhere how many people must be on the bridge or what their qualifications must be. The regulation sets out the composition of the "deck watch." Many people have taken this to mean the "bridge watch," but this is not so. The Crewing Regulations define "watch, in respect of a ship," as "(a) that part of the complement that is required for the purpose of attending to the *navigation or security* of the ship" (emphasis added).

The responsibilities of the deck watch are not limited to the bridge; there is much more involved in operating a ship. Security is one example of the major duties. There is often a need for an officer to attend to matters off the bridge. A primary reason for having two officers on duty is to make this possible.

Also from the Crewing Regulations:

> (4) The additional person and the second additional person are not each required, in respect of one of the deck watches in any 24-hour period, to hold the certificate referred to in paragraph (2)(b) or (c) [i.e., efficient deckhand certificate, an able seaman certificate or a bridge watchman certificate] if either the additional person or the second additional person, but not both, is assigned to that deck watch as a rating under training for the purpose of obtaining the certificate.

So, to summarize, the regulations require that two people in the deck watch—*not* the bridge watch—hold an efficient deckhand certificate, an able seaman certificate, or a bridge watchman certificate. This requirement was met. The regulations do not state that anyone is to be supervised at all times or at any time.

All of which is academic. The bridge watchman certificate, like the able seaman certificate and the efficient deckhand certificate, does not qualify one to navigate or to monitor navigation. Neither does it, or any other certificate, certify that the holder is conversant with the idiosyncrasies of the *Queen of the North*'s unique systems. The exam for the bridge watchman certificate asks questions about such things as sewing canvas and handling cargo.

The bridge team of the *Queen of the North* on March 22, 2006, comprised experienced seamen whose qualifications met the requirements of the regulations. The Second Mate had served with BC Ferries since 1980, had obtained his watchkeeping mate, ship certificate in 1997, and had been relieving as third and fourth mate since 1998. He obtained his first mate, intermediate voyage certificate in 2001 and had sailed regularly as second mate. He was fully qualified, experienced, trustworthy, and completely at home with being in charge on the bridge or on the deck.

Although the Fourth Mate had less seniority than the Second Mate, and his title might have had an inferior ring to it, his qualifications were in no way inferior. He was a fully qualified navigator with experience nearly equal to that of the Second Mate. He held a certificate of competency as second mate, valid for any size of ship, and he had, in fact, sailed as second mate. Personnel with the same qualifications, and many with less experience, sail regularly as second mates throughout the BC Ferries fleet. Some have sailed regularly as first mates in major vessels, including the *Queen of the North* and the *Queen of Prince Rupert*.

In the case of the Quartermaster, it was established that she was technically qualified to be in that position. The Divisional Inquiry noted that she "had enough sea time to write the bridge watchman's exam, although at the time of the incident had not yet written the exam and was considered to be a 'rating under training.'"[12] She had been off sick for several days, so had not had much experience with the new steering system.

All of us in the *Queen of the North*'s bridge team were faced with changes made to critical bridge equipment since we were last on board. The four mates and I received a briefing from the off-going "A" crew, who had brought the ship out of refit and who also had to contend with these changes. On the basis of the briefing we received, we were tasked with having to familiarize ourselves with the new gear as well as familiarizing the eight quartermasters with those aspects that they would be required to operate. The changeover from autopilot to manual steering and back was not a function that they would be carrying out—this was for the mates or the master. The only change in the equipment that they would be operating was in one of the two steering wheels. One of them, the forward steering wheel, was unchanged in its operation. But the aft steering wheel was modified so that its operation was the same as the forward wheel. In other words, the two were standardized. The Quartermaster had said that she was "a bit nervous"

. . . .

12   Divisional Inquiry, 11.

about this new equipment.[13] In response to this, extra time was spent explaining the use of the new steering wheel (identical to the existing forward steering wheel), and an off-duty quartermaster was brought up to stand by her as she steered the ship out of port. The off-duty quartermaster gave his input as required and was ready to step in if she became overwhelmed. Given the satisfactory way she steered the ship through the narrow channel that leads out of Prince Rupert, and her performance in steering the ship across the remainder of Chatham Sound, there was no evident reason to prevent her from performing her assigned duties.

The bridge team composition was appropriate up until the time the ship encountered restricted visibility and lost an important radar target. When the situation changed, the Second Mate was needed. If Lilgert had correctly understood his situation and his need for help, he would have called Keven Hilton. Again, the real issue was his failure to assess the situation correctly and understand that he was getting into trouble. This is a failure of perception but not a lapse of principles.

MUSIC ON THE BRIDGE

Both the TSB and DI reports mention the fact that music was audible on radio calls between the *Queen of the North* and Prince Rupert. The DI report gives this as evidence of a casual watchstanding behaviour.[14] Similarly, the Workers' Compensation Appeal Tribunal noted that "the DI report also observed that a casual watchkeeping behaviour was practiced at times when operating the ship, based on evidence at the DI proceedings and further demonstrated by music playing on the bridge as overheard on radio calls." Further, according to the WCAT, "Captain C[apacci] testified that one of the contributing factors that led the employer to lose confidence in the worker as a Master was that according to Captain F[randsen], the worker permitted a radio to play music in the wheelhouse when the ship was underway, disagreeing with Captain F's view on the practice,"[15] namely, that music was a sign of casual watchkeeping.

· · · · · · · · · · · ·

13   Divisional Inquiry, 11, 12.

14   Divisional Inquiry, 24.

15   WCAT Decision, 4, 49.

Many members of the public seemed to think that the playing of music, as well as the conversation between the two crew members on the bridge, indicated that something other than navigation was taking place.

However, this view of music and conversation as a problem and, presumably, a distraction, flies in the face of scientific research on the effects of fatigue and how to manage them. The majority of the world's ships operate around the clock, which means, obviously, that there must be crew on duty around the clock. Up until fairly recent times, the question of fatigue was largely ignored. An ability to manage with a reduced level of sleep, whether in terms of actual time spent sleeping or the quality of that sleep, was for too long seen as a sign of toughness. Today, shift-workers who deny the serious effects of fatigue will find themselves in the minority. Many are looking for practical advice to help deal with these effects.

One group that has been helpful in this area is the International Maritime Organization (IMO), the United Nations' specialized agency responsible for improving maritime safety and preventing pollution from ships. In 2001 it published *IMO Circular 1014, Guidance on Fatigue Mitigation and Management,* which made numerous recommendations on fatigue mitigation:

> The most powerful means of relieving fatigue is to get proper sleep and to rest when appropriate. However, a number of things have been identified as potentially providing some short-term relief. Note, however, that these countermeasures may simply mask the symptoms temporarily—the fatigue has not been eliminated ...
>
> • Bright lights, cool dry air, music and other irregular sounds can increase alertness ...
> • Social interaction (conversation) can help you stay awake. However, the interaction must be active to be effective. [16]

• • • • • • • • • • •

16   IMO, "Guidance on Fatigue Management and Mitigation," MSC/Circ. 1014 (London: IMO, June 12, 2001), 16, 25. Available online at http://www.imo.org/en/OurWork /HumanElement/VisionPrinciplesGoals/Pages/Fatigue.aspx

The question of whether to allow conversation and music in a working environment, particularly aboard ship, has been controversial. In my earlier days with the Northern Service, I had the privilege of sailing with the great captain Dave Perry. His standing orders stipulated that when the engine telegraph was set to "Standby" (signifying a need for heightened alertness), all conversation not related to navigation was to stop. While I never actually included this in my own standing orders, I believed it was a very good policy, and I made it a practice to keep all the conversation focused. I have sailed with captains who allowed no unrelated conversation at any time, and it was a miserable experience for all involved.

Over the years I have allowed some music to be played, quietly, some of the time, on the bridge. Those times would be restricted to the most open stretches of water and the best of navigational conditions. Personally, I would not condone music being played during radio communications, and members of my regular watch, the "A" crew, would know that, but the fact Lilgert left it on is not by itself very compelling evidence of casual watchkeeping by the "B" crew.

FORMALITY ON THE BRIDGE

When interviewed at the Divisional Inquiry, the regular master of "B" crew (the crew of the ship on the night of the sinking) commented on a lack of formality and speculated that this contributed to the grounding.[17] Both the DI and the TSB included this opinion in their reports, and the TSB described it as either a "contributing factor" to or a "cause" of the grounding.[18] I refer to it as opinion because the regular master was not on board the week of the sinking, and he cannot say how the crew acted under my command. Trafford Taylor did not call me a "Bridge Nazi" because I was known for more relaxed navigational practices than other masters.[19]

None of the critics have indicated what value, if any, formality would have brought to the bridge and exactly what value was lost without it. Formality on its own avails nothing but formality. "Protocol" and

• • • • • • • • • • • •

17 WCAT Decision, 37–38.

18 Divisional Inquiry, 24; TSB Report, 40, 51, 53.

19 WCAT Decision, 31.

"procedure," when applied correctly, are an important part of the crew's functionality. In fact, the much-lauded Bridge Resource Management (BRM) philosophy invariably points out that formality is often an impediment to teamwork. Aviation's Crew Resource Management (CRM) also makes this point. Both BRM and CRM make specific reference to accidents occurring because a culture of formality gave junior members the feeling that it was not their place to give input.

It is interesting to trace the journey of one word of opinion as it meanders through various dissertations and grows incrementally from a "lack of formality" to "accepted principles of navigation safety were not consistently or rigorously applied." From there, it grows to become "Unsafe navigation practices persisted … " And the next increment takes it to "that, in this occurrence, contributed to the loss of situational awareness by the bridge team."

And so, from one word of speculative hearsay, a case arises that informality sank the ship.

There is no evidence that "unsafe navigation practices persisted." But the allegation laid the foundation for the Workers' Compensation Appeal Tribunal, which used the same incremental method to uphold my firing. WCAT's incremental method brought it to these rhetorical questions: How could there have been a complete breakdown in a watch organization? And why did I never mention this complete breakdown at the Divisional Inquiry?

I didn't mention it at the Divisional Inquiry because there wasn't a speck of real evidence presented pointing to any breakdown in organization beyond the fact the officer of the watch lost situational awareness.

CHAPTER 9

MUST THE CAPTAIN GO DOWN WITH THE SHIP?

THIS IS THE SEQUENCE OF EVENTS CONCERNING MY DISMISSAL FROM BC Ferries and my fight to keep my job.

1. On January 11, 2007, I was fired.
2. I filed a complaint under Section 151 of the *Workers' Compensation Act*.
3. On July 21, 2008, I won.
4. I was reinstated.
5. On March 11, 2010, BC Ferries won on appeal to the Workers' Compensation Appeal Tribunal.
6. I was fired again.
7. On April 1, 2011, I lost a judicial review in the British Columbia Supreme Court.
8. On November 24, 2011, I lost on appeal to the British Columbia Court of Appeal.

It was five years of demoralizing struggle that left my career and finances in disarray. A good question to ask is why would a taxpayer-supported public service organization like BC Ferries do this to an employee with nineteen years of exemplary service, whom they repeatedly said they did not blame for the accident and, indeed, praised for his role in directing the rescue of the ship's company?

A marine lawyer named Darren Williams published an article in *Western Mariner* in January 2012, shortly after I had lost my appeal to be reinstated under the *Workers' Compensation Act*. He provided an accurate précis of the BC Ferries position, titled "Must the Captain Always Go Down with His Ship?" He was speaking metaphorically, of course, but it was a perceptive comment on what might have been the single most successful of many reasons put forward by BC Ferries: that the captain must take the rap, even if he was not directly involved in the mishap. I will have more to say about that in Chapter 10, but for now, here is Williams' paraphrase of the case against me:

> The master, who had rightfully been in his cabin when the grounding occurred, said he was unable to explain why the vessel failed to change course. During this inquiry the master was asked to list serious safety concerns that might have caused the vessel to go aground and provide a list of safety concerns that BC Ferries had not responded to previously. The master provided a list of issues he had noted over the years, but it was agreed none of these caused or contributed to the sinking.[1]

That is the BC Ferries version. My version is that I did not agree that none of those issues caused or contributed to the sinking. I had already said that I did not know what caused the grounding (the possible scenario described in Chapter 6 is one I developed after learning more about what was happening on the bridge from Karl Lilgert's and Karen Briker's testimony in court in 2013). Several of the issues I raised, such as the substandard radar, ambiguous compass information, and ambiguities in the autopilot and steering system, might very well have contributed to the sinking. Two of the issues did cause problems after the grounding (echo sounder problems and the history of inaccurate passenger information).

I had to take all of BC Ferries' evolving reasons for firing me with deadly seriousness because my career and livelihood depended on my ability to refute them. Additionally, a number of august bodies, such as the Supreme Court of BC, appeared to be siding with BC Ferries, so I was forced to wrestle with each new rationale in turn.

• • • • • • • • • • • •

1   Darren Williams, "Must the Captain Always Go Down with the Ship?" *Western Mariner*, January 2012, available at http://www.leaguelaw.com/posts /must-captain-always-go-ship/

The first reason BC Ferries gave for firing me was the most easily refuted. As WCB case officer Elaine Murray reported in her decision of July 21, 2008, a BC Ferries executive vice president wrote to me on January 15, 2007, and said, "After reviewing your status relative to the company's operational and staff requirements we have concluded that your services will not be required in the future."[2] BC Ferries itself withdrew this reason, admitting it was false and saying it had been only been trying to "soften the blow." It seems Ms. Murray didn't entirely buy that, as she wrote,

> The employer acknowledges that it was not honest in the January 15, 2007 letter as to why it was terminating the worker. I accept that it was not honest at that time, given that "operational and staff requirements" were clearly not the reason for letting the worker go. The employer needed Exempt Masters and advertised as such just days before it officially fired the worker. Unfortunately, it is not that unusual for an employer's firing of an employee to have an air of dishonesty. Sometimes an employer is genuinely trying to "soften the blow" to the employee; whereas, at other times, an employer's motives are more self-serving such that they are more concerned with avoiding how uncomfortable it can be for them to be honest. Furthermore, an employer may attempt to "manage" the legal liability that can arise from a decision to terminate an employee. By not being forthcoming, they hope that the employee will go away quietly. This frequently leads to employees being unable to understand why they have been fired, especially when they are fired without cause.
>
> At issue is whether the employer is now being entirely honest about its reasons for firing the worker, in the face

· · · · · · · · · · · ·

2   Workers' Compensation Board, "Worker Complaint of Discriminatory Action Decision (*Workers Compensation Act*, Sections 150, 151, 152, and 153)," Reference 2008D007 (July 21, 2008), 12 (hereafter WCB Decision). I obtained a copy of the report for publication through the Freedom of Information Act, which meant some content was "severed" because its disclosure would "unreasonably invade the personal privacy of third parties." I have indicated missing text with the notation "(redacted passage)."

of the discriminatory action complaint. I accept that it is no longer trying to "soften the blow", and that it is being more forthcoming about its reasons.[3]

Are case officers ever tempted to be ironic, in their ever-so-dry fashion? Because once we filed our complaint, BC Ferries shifted from trying to soften the blow to coming at me with everything they had. In our submission, my lawyer, Howard Ehrlich, had referred to the fact that the Divisional Inquiry found no fault with me. Howard stated that I was "exonerated" by the report. BC Ferries responded, "He is in error. In fact, there are specific issues identified which relate to his performance as ship's Master. These issues, among others discussed below, were of such nature that [the employer] lost confidence in the Complainant's ability to command. As a result, the decision was taken to terminate his employment."

Murray continued, "The employer then set out the seven numbered reasons supporting its decision to dismiss the worker."[4]

The seven reasons cited by BC Ferries almost entirely relate to issues aired at the Divisional Inquiry and my responses to them, many of which we have already thoroughly discussed. They are:

1. The Divisional Inquiry report concluded that the navigational watch failed to maintain a proper lookout by all available means ...

2. The Divisional Inquiry report concluded that a casual watch standing behaviour was practised at times when operating the ferry vessel, based on evidence from the Senior Master (Captain F) and further demonstrated by music playing on the bridge (overheard on radio calls) ...

3. The Divisional Inquiry found three challenges with the cabin sweep: (1) the absence of a cabin assignment list; (2) multiple pass keys were required to open passenger staterooms and crew cabins; and (3) once a cabin was entered and searched, the door should

3   WCB Decision, 23.
4   WCB Decision, 24.

be marked with chalk to indicate that it is clear. But chalk could not be located ...

4. The ship's log book was left behind, which is a significant breach of a Master's responsibility ...

5. The worker had countermanded the Senior Master's orders with respect to certain of the controls on the bridge ...

6. According to the employer, the Master is always on duty, and the actions of those under his command remain his responsibility at all times. In the employer's view, the worker "did not seem to appreciate his responsibilities in this regard and this necessarily contributed to [the employer's] loss of confidence in his abilities" ...

7. The worker's suggestion in his submission that he was completely exonerated is ... (redacted passage) The employer then explained as follows:

> This attitude was noted by those members of the Divisional Inquiry who are senior representatives of [the company's] management team. In short, they found the Complainant to lack a proper appreciation of his own role as part of that management team. Moreover, he demonstrated no contrition or remorse, he failed to accept any personal responsibility and appeared far more concerned with self-preservation than with recognizing or appreciating his role as Master of the vessel. Frankly, the perceptions and concerns of senior personnel in this regard were not alleviated by the Complainant's arrival at the Divisional Inquiry with the Union's legal representative in tow.[5]

• • • • • • • • • • • •

5   In fact, I was exercising my right to have counsel. As I've mentioned, Jack Buchan was with me because I was a member of the Canadian Merchant Service Guild.

> In short, [the employer] lost confi-
> dence in the Complainant's ability to
> serve as Master of a vessel.[6]

Before going into the case officer's responses to these seven sins cited by BC Ferries, I would like to point out that they are hardly deadly. There is no drunkenness while on duty, no molestation of colleagues, not even a simple case of ordering the wrong course or forgetting a procedural step. It is all very iffy and indirect—things other people did while I was asleep, chalk I provided but someone else removed, papers another officer dropped in order to rescue a shipmate, and perfectly legitimate actions by me, such as appearing with a lawyer, that senior managers nevertheless took exception to, etc.

Elaine Murray, for one, was not impressed, pointing out that the reasons given were not very persuasive considering that "the employer had confidence in the worker, such that it promoted him to Exempt Master in February 2006. At that time, the employer characterized the worker's performance as being 'more than satisfactory', not simply 'satisfactory' as described in its submission on this complaint."[7]

Ms. Murray then dealt with each of the company complaints in succession:

> It is abundantly clear from both the Divisional Inquiry and the TSB that the cause of this accident was the bridge crew's failure to make the necessary course change because it was not following sound watch keeping practices that evening. The employer contends that this failure (the first and second of its seven reasons) caused it to lose confidence in the worker. Although I agree with the premise that a Master of a vessel is always on duty, I fail to see what, if anything, the worker could have done in these circumstances. There is no compelling evidence that another Master would have acted differently.
>
> It is only reasonable that the worker was asleep in his

. . . .

6   WCB Decision, 15–18.

7   WCB Decision, 24.

quarters when the QN [*Queen of the North*] struck Gil Island, having left the vessel in what he and the employer understood to be qualified and capable crew hands, with standing orders and night orders to call him if needed. On a ship sailing 24 hours a day, there are times when the Master must delegate the navigation to certified officers, which is what the worker did.

While recognizing that the worker's usual crew was not aboard the QN, I accept that the worker was likely unaware of B watch's overly casual practice of watch standing behaviour without the Senior Master of "B" watch having informed him. Nor is it likely that the worker was aware of the nature of the relationship between the 4/O and the QM1. Yet, even if he was, he ought to have been able to count on the crew being professional and keeping a safe watch.[8]

As for the missing chalk:

In addition to human error on the part of the bridge crew, the Divisional Inquiry and the TSB identified some systemic problems, which were the employer's responsibility to resolve. I also fail to see how the blame for these problems could be laid at the worker's feet. In particular, I am puzzled how the employer could even suggest the third reason (the challenges with cabin sweep given the absence of a cabin assignment list, the need for multiple pass keys, and no chalk to mark searched cabins, which are all company procedural issues) to explain why it lost confidence in the worker's abilities as a Master. The items listed in the third reason are the employer's responsibility, fleet-wide.[9]

She was right; it was the company's responsibility, and both Transport Canada and I had been requesting a proper evacuation plan for some

. . . .

8   WCB Decision, 24–25.

9   WCB Decision, 25.

time.[10] Had I not taken it upon myself to draft cabin search procedures and all the other emergency procedures—and drilled the crew in their execution—only the launching procedures would have been routine; every other aspect of the evacuation would have been left to improvisation. In all likelihood, it was this planning that saved BC Ferries from having a far more serious tragedy to deal with.

Murray did not buy the loss of the log book as a firing issue either:

> The employer's fourth reason (leaving the log book behind) is also puzzling, given that the worker understood that ... (redacted passage) had the log books. Unfortunately, while in the process of dealing with a ... (redacted passage) [the person] left the log books behind. Surely the worker was entitled to rely on his subordinates in this situation. Or, is the employer suggesting that the Master cannot rely on his crew for anything? I am of the view that making an issue out of the loss of the log books is just another weak attempt by the employer to bolster its position that it lost confidence in the worker.[11]

Murray allowed that BC Ferries "may have formed an impression, rightly or wrongly, that the worker was not deserving of its confidence because casual watch standing behaviour went on (1st and 2nd reasons) and the worker allowed the watch to manage certain controls contrary to the senior master's orders (5th reason). On the other hand, as earlier stated, short of remaining on the bridge 24 hours a day, the worker had to have faith in his bridge crew, not only to do their jobs, but to notify him in case of concern, as per his orders."[12]

· · · · · · · · · · · ·

10   This is noted in Attachment 20(b) of the Divisional Inquiry, a Marine Safety Notice from Transport Canada, dated March 2, 2006, that includes as deficiencies: "Vessel requires a TCMS approved lifesaving plan" and "Vessel requires to have an evacuation plan/procedure." BC Ferries Divisional Inquiry "*Queen of the North* Grounding and Sinking: Attachments," DI #815-06-01 (Victoria: BC Ferries, 2007), http://www.bcferries.com/about/qnorthdivisionalinquiry.html

11   WCB Decision, 25.

12   WCB Decision, 25.

All of this was somewhat beside the point in terms of our complaint, however, which was based on Howard's argument that if the decision to fire me was influenced even in some small way by my bringing up safety issues at the DI, this would "taint" the decision under Section 151 of the *Workers' Compensation Act*, and my firing would be illegal.

The company denied that my raising what it called a "litany of safety issues" had the slightest influence on their decision to fire me,[13] but they were undone in part by their own clever arguments—at least in this round.

"This brings us to the employer's sixth and seventh reasons for dismissing the worker," Murray wrote, "which, in my view, go to the crux of this matter."

> In a nutshell, as the employer submits, management perceived an "attitude" from the worker during the Divisional Inquiry, which led it to lose confidence in him. So, what was the employer's perception of his attitude, and was it in any way connected to his raising of safety complaints?
>
> The employer's evidence provides the answer. Its comments about the worker's attitude during the Divisional Inquiry make it clear that, at least in part, the worker demonstrated an attitude of not being "part of the management team". In other words, he was not yet one of them; rather, he still perceived himself (in the employer's view) as being part of the union.[14]

Murray was quick to dismiss the company position that there was something wrong with my appearing at the DI with legal representation: "I am mindful that the lawyer 'in tow' was from the Canadian Merchant Service Guild, which represents exempt and non-exempt Masters, among others ... The employer's criticism of the worker having representation in something as serious as a Divisional Inquiry into the sinking of one of its vessels, on which the worker was the Master, suggests to me that it should be far more troubled by its own attitude about union and management than that of the worker."[15]

. . . .

13   WCB Decision, 26.

14   WCB Decision, 26.

15   WCB Decision, 26.

She saw the company's objection to my using the same lawyer as the union as a clue to the company's attitude, making a connection between the union and safety: "Given the employer's evidence of the clear dichotomy it sees between union and management, I am left to ponder whether safety issues and concerns would or would not transcend this divide for the employer. At this point, what I see as the key issue is whether the worker's voicing of safety concerns played a role in management deciding that he was not a management team player, and thus firing him."[16]

She referred to "Review of Operational Safety at British Columbia Ferry Services Inc.," the January 2007 report by former BC auditor general George Morfitt, noting that he had highlighted a "largely dysfunctional" employer / union relationship that posed a "significant impediment to resolving operational safety issues."[17]

"Mr. Morfitt's conclusions about the lack of cooperation between union and management in the workplace with respect to safety concerns resonate here," she found, adding,

> In my view, the evidence suggests that at least part of the employer's reasons for expecting the worker to have an "appreciation of his role on the management team" stems from it not understanding (at least before the Morfitt report) that safety concerns are not to be divided along lines of management or union.
>
> My impression from the employer's evidence is that once an employee was in management, the expectation was that the management employee would approach safety concerns from a different perspective or in a different manner. My impression stems partly from Captain T's final comments to the worker during the May 25, 2006 Divisional Inquiry when, after the worker had outlined how he thought safety matters could be better handled, Captain T asked him if he still wanted to work for the company. This comment, which I consider to be illuminating, left me with the definite impression that at least part of

· · · · · · · · · · · ·

16 WCB Decision, 26.
17 WCB Decision, 27.

the worker's "attitude" and failure to demonstrate "proper appreciation of his own role as part of the management team", which led to the senior management terminating him, stemmed from his voicing concerns about safety and suggestions on improving safety during the Divisional Inquiry.

My impression also stems from Captain T's comments to the worker during his first interview with the Divisional Inquiry, where he asked why the worker would have taken the job of Master, given the number of safety concerns that he had. On the one hand, I have no doubt that Captain T was genuinely looking for evidence of any safety concerns, especially ones that may have caused or contributed to the QN sinking. On the other hand, when the worker discussed some of his concerns, Captain T ... (redacted passage) and questioned him along the lines of why he took the job in the first place and whether he even wanted to work for the company. Again, I find Captain T's comments to be most telling.[18]

Elaine Murray, a lawyer and long-time WCB official who would later move to the WCAT herself, concluded that my firing was indeed tainted by the company's reaction to my safety concerns, and found in my favour. She gave us a chance to mediate a remedy. When that went nowhere, on February 23, 2009, she ordered that BC Ferries reinstate me to my position as exempt master no later than May 25, 2009, and that the company attempt to reach an agreement on the amount of wages and benefits I had lost, with interest owing, no later than May 25, 2009. It was like a dream come true. My family and I felt the dark clouds of the sinking clear off for the first time in two years. Life was suddenly full of promise once again.

But Howard warned me that BC Ferries would likely appeal, and it did.

The WCAT took a long time, holding ten days of hearings from June through November 2009 and delivering its decision on March 11, 2010—two years after the original WCB hearing and four years after the sinking. With that, the dark clouds came back and stayed.

. . . .

18   WCB Decision, 27–28.

The WCAT was heard by three vice-chairs—Heather McDonald, Leslie Christensen, and Warren Hoole—all Workers' Compensation veterans, and Trafford Taylor and George Capacci spoke for BC Ferries. I didn't testify.

The WCAT didn't uncover substantial new evidence missed in the original complaint; instead, it mainly viewed the old evidence differently.

On the issue of "the deck watch failing to maintain a proper lookout by all available means; and the DI report's finding that a casual watchkeeping behaviour was practiced ... on the night in question,"[19] the WCAT apparently had no problem accepting this as fact on the evidence of a man who wasn't even on board the *Queen of the North* on March 22, 2006. At the DI, Don Frandsen, the regular captain of "B" crew, had criticized his crew's navigational practices.[20] At least in part because of Frandsen's testimony, the Divisional Inquiry, the TSB, and the WCAT concluded that a prime cause of the accident must have been these "poor navigational practices." Because I did not also name these alleged problems as a cause of the accident, I was accused of being uncooperative at the DI.[21] The WCAT seemed to accept the company position that failing to endorse problems I didn't believe in meant I was failing in my responsibility as captain and gave BC Ferries management a valid reason for losing confidence in me as an exempt Master.[22]

On the issue of "challenges with the cabin sweep (absence of a passenger cabin assignment list, absence of chalk to mark cabin and stateroom doors; the fact that multiple pass keys were required to open staterooms and cabins)," the WCAT agreed with Elaine Murray that these were all company procedural issues, but still found reason to lay it at my doorstep because of the company's "firm position that a Master is responsible for everything that goes wrong on his or her ship."[23] An irony here is that there might have been no keys at all if I hadn't taken on the responsibility of assembling and placing them in a special box myself, along with chalk, which had disappeared during the recent refit.

My failure to take the log book ashore, which the company had called

· · · · · · · · · · · ·

19   WCAT Decision, 67.

20   WCAT Decision, 37, 47–49.

21   WCAT Decision, 59.

22   WCAT Decision, 67.

23   WCAT Decision, 68.

"a significant breach of the master's responsibility" in its submission to the WCB,[24] was dialled back at the WCAT to "one small matter [that] would not cause them to lose confidence in the worker." Nevertheless, the WCAT came to the company's defence, saying "this issue was raised in the employer's submissions to the Board largely to demonstrate that the worker's performance as Master was not 'perfect.'"[25]

The WCAT's position on the charge of countermanding the senior master's bridge orders was curious. What WCAT is referring to was not a bridge order but a document titled "Changeover Procedures," which Frandsen had posted in the wheelhouse. It set out one of a number of procedures that could be used with the autopilot/steering system. Capacci and Taylor apparently agreed that the procedures the "B" crew officers and I chose to use for operating the new steering mode switch were simpler than those posted by the senior master and "may well have been better." When would simpler not be better, especially in the haphazard arrangement of the *Queen of the North*'s bridge? That still didn't let me off the hook, however, because I didn't consult with the senior master and/or the marine superintendent and post new instructions on the bulkhead before approving this simpler process.[26] This was brand new gear we were just getting used to, and we would have done the consulting and posting in due time.

The crucial accusation, however, was that I tried to "defray responsibility for the incident."[27] The WCAT recorded that "Captain C testified that in failing to focus on matters such as navigational issues, watchkeeping practices, or crew assignment, the worker was essentially implying that the loss of the ship was not his fault or responsibility."[28] It also noted that "one of the reasons given by Captain C for losing confidence in the worker ... is Captain C's perception that *at no time* after the loss of the ship did the worker show any introspection or self-questioning about his role in the accident and whether he could have done anything differently to prevent the tragedy ... Captain C referred to several other marine incidents, not

. . . .

24   WCB Decision, 16.

25   WCAT Decision, 68.

26   WCAT Decision, 45, 49–50, 58, 69.

27   Williams, "Must the Captain Always Go Down with the Ship?"

28   WCAT Decision, 54.

of the same magnitude as the case at hand, in which the Masters of the ships ... engaged in a process of self-questioning about how they might have done things in a better way" (emphasis added).[29]

Introspection is the examination of one's own thoughts. Self-questioning is the process of questioning one's self. These processes do not involve anyone else. As a professional, I engage in self-questioning every day, good and bad. Capacci was with me on only two occasions after the accident: at the DI interrogations. He knew nothing about my introspection or self-questioning.[30]

When asked, at the WCAT hearing, how I seemed when I was met in Hartley Bay, Trafford Taylor told the Tribunal that I seemed not to understand what happened, I displayed no sense of loss.[31] Another observer at the time saw it quite differently:

> Shortly after 10 AM, all the survivors were onboard the Sir Wilfred Laurier, headed toward Prince Rupert. There was one man left behind, though: the still unnamed, skipper of the Queen of the North.
>
> "He was a sad guy," said Karen Clifford,[32] who remembers a silent, forlorn figure amongst the survivors.
>
> "He looked sad. I felt sorry for him. He flew out about 20 minutes later by helicopter, after all the others had left. BC Ferries sent in somebody to take him home, I guess."[33]

• • • • • • • • • • • •

29 WCAT Decision, 30.

30 Ironically, during a short break in the WCAT proceedings, Capacci began to talk about Captain Sullenberger, the pilot who ditched his disabled airliner in the Hudson River, saying that this was his idea of a captain and "I would fly with him anywhere." Capacci might be surprised to read this account in the *New York Daily News*: "'That pilot is a stud,' said one police source. 'After the crash, he was sitting there in the ferry terminal, wearing his hat, sipping his coffee and acting like nothing happened'" (Alison Endar, Larry McShane, Geoff Gillette, "Hero of the Hudson: Pilot of US Airways Flight 1549 Saved Every Passenger with Miracle Landing," *New York Daily News*, January 16, 2009).

31 WCAT Decision, 30.

32 Band Manager, Hartley Bay Indian Reserve.

33 "Anatomy of a Rescue," *Vancouver Sun*, March 23, 2006.

And although the WCAT acknowledged, quoting from an earlier decision, that "neither I nor anyone else can accurately discern the 'true motives' of the employer,"[34] both the tribunal and the employer seemed to feel they could accurately discern *my* motives and thought processes. The WCAT Decision includes the following statement:

> In final argument the worker's position was that there was no evidentiary foundation whatsoever for the employer's perception that the worker did not seem to appreciate his responsibilities as Master. We disagree. It is true that nowhere in the evidence is there any reference to a verbal or written statement by the worker expressly communicating that he was not sorry about the loss of the ship and two lives or that he refused to take any responsibility for the incident or that he did not wonder what he could have done differently that might have prevented the accident. But the evidence also reveals that at no time did the worker ever verbally or in writing express those sentiments to Captain C or Captain T or for that matter, to anyone in the employer's management ... It is sufficient to state that the worker did not offer to resign, nor did he express to the employer's management any words that they expected or would like to have heard from him about his role as Master of the ship and his acceptance of personal accountability for the tragedy.[35]

In the days that followed the sinking, top BC Ferries executives moved to "accept responsibility" for the accident. At the Divisional Inquiry, Trafford Taylor said, "I accept full responsibility." George Capacci, on the morning of the sinking, offered his resignation because, he testified, he felt responsible for the situation.[36] It was not accepted, and the offer was used at the WCAT hearing as an example of how to accept responsibility. Captain Don Frandsen, senior master at the time, apparently "second-

. . . .

34   WCAT Decision, 17.

35   WCAT Decision, 31.

36   WCAT Decision, 28.

guessed himself and kept wondering what else he could have done to prevent the tragedy," and he too offered his resignation, which was also not accepted.[37] In an interview with BC *Business* magazine, David Hahn claimed, "As the CEO, you're ultimately responsible. It's non-negotiable in terms of whose responsibility it is. I mean the whole thing."[38]

One of the reasons given for firing me was that I showed "no remorse or contrition."[39] Every dictionary I consulted associates those words with guilt. No one said I was guilty; on the contrary, people on all sides were thanking me for my handling of the incident and calling me a hero. I was inwardly devastated by the event but it is my nature as well as my training to maintain composure during a crisis. Perhaps my critics read this as lack of concern but I felt I had demonstrated my concern through my actions. I was also in a fundamentally different position than those others expressing remorse and accepting responsibility. I was being named in multiple lawsuits and was under legal advice not to say anything that might prejudice my position—or my employer's position.

The WCAT spent much of its time going over my behaviour at the Divisional Inquiry and decided that I had given Taylor and Capacci sufficient reason to justify firing me without involving my safety concerns. WCAT contended that my belief I was fired for raising safety concerns was "inconsistent with the fact that [I] had raised the same types of safety concerns in the years before [I] was promoted … to the position of exempt Master."[40]

"Exempt" means exempt from union membership. More correctly, I became *excluded* from union membership. This means that during my previous nineteen years of raising safety concerns, I had the protection of the union. The very first time I raised a safety concern without that protection, they fired me.

The WCAT Decision makes much of the fact that, according to BC Ferries, I "lacked a proper appreciation of the role on the management team of exempt Master."[41] According to Capacci, I was to view him as my

. . . .

37   WCAT Decision, 29.

38   Gary Manson, "David Hahn: Play It as It Lays," BC *Business,* May 1, 2007, http://www
.bcbusiness.ca/people/david-hahn-play-it-as-it-lays

39   WCAT Decision, 25.

40   WCAT Decision, 57.

41   WCAT Decision, 32.

"union representative," which meant I didn't need legal representation at the DI. "I was his representative," Capacci told the WCAT. "I was looking out for his best interests and to make sure that we got to the facts ... I expected him to fully participate in the DI to find out what happened." His view was "that the employer's management team is a very close group who are expected to turn to each other for help and advice, not to outsiders such as unions or similar associations." Apparently the fact that I appeared with Jack Buchan "insulted" Capacci. The WCAT notes that he was "the same legal counsel, J, who had earlier represented the witnesses who refused to testify at the DI proceedings about key events before the ship grounded," and Taylor "was irritated that J's presence might be a signal that the worker, another key witness, was also going to refuse to testify on important matters."[42]

And although the WCAT admitted that "the employer's Fleet Regulations acknowledge the right of DI witnesses including exempt and non-exempt Masters to have representation at DI proceedings" and that "the written notice/request ... to the worker to attend the DI stated that he was entitled to bring 'Union or other representation' to the DI proceedings if he wished," it concluded that "by bringing a lawyer to the DI interview, the worker was betraying one of the employer's core values and also going against the employer's management style," and "lacked a proper appreciation of his role of exempt Master as part of the employer's management team."[43]

The tribunal went on to compare my testimony to that of Captain Frandsen, the senior master on the Northern routes and the regular master on "B" crew. It noted that Frandsen criticized the crew, focusing on "a general problem with watchkeeping and casual bridge crew practices," and stating that "B" crew was a "worry."[44] The tribunal also noted that Frandsen named me as one of the masters who allowed an informal atmosphere on the bridge and who changed his standing orders.[45]

That was a bit much. I stand on my reputation of being an exacting captain. Even the WCAT recorded, on no less an authority than Trafford

. . . .

42   WCAT Decision, 33, 34, 35.

43   WCAT Decision, 35–36.

44   WCAT Decision, 47, 48.

45   WCAT Decision, 49.

Taylor, that I was "a Master who was severe in bridge discipline."[46] I allowed music to be played, with certain restrictions, because I believe in its restorative powers (as I have discussed in Chapter 8).

The people playing music while I slept during the night of March 21, 2006, were members of the crew that had been supervised for five years by the very man levelling the charge against me—Don Frandsen.

According to the WCAT report, Frandsen told the DI about "long-standing practices of shouting political arguments, heated arguments and music on the bridge" that "in five years as Master of B watch he had failed [to stop]."[47] This is quite a remarkable revelation, and he had never mentioned it when he handed his crew over to me. Throughout the short time they were under my command, I never saw "B" crew indulge in the kind of behaviour that Frandsen described. As far as I was concerned, they demonstrated that they were competent sailors. Never was this more apparent than during the magnificent job they had all done rescuing passengers and injured shipmates on the night of March 22, 2006.

The WCAT stated that the "safety concern about poor navigational practices raised by Captain F[randsen] would be much more embarrassing to the employer ... Yet the employer did not retaliate against Captain F for expressing his safety concern."[48] Since Frandsen was not fired, the tribunal reasoned that BC Ferries did want to hear about safety issues and would not discriminate against those who brought them up. But when Frandsen was asked the same question that got me in so much trouble—namely, "had [he] ever been turned down by management when he had requested safety equipment"—he said "no."[49]

As WCAT notes, Frandsen did bring up embarrassing safety concerns at the DI, but there is an essential difference between the kinds of safety concerns he discussed and those that I discussed. His concerns mainly faulted other workers and supported the theory that the accident was caused by employee negligence. The WCAT implies the same thing: "Although the DI panel suspected poor watchkeeping, it lacked concrete evidence about any

. . . .

46 WCAT Decision, 49.

47 WCAT Decision, 48.

48 WCAT Decision, 53.

49 WCAT Decision, 47.

cause of the accident ... In this context, we find that DI panel members expected to hear helpful information from the worker in his role as the ship's Master on the voyage, particularly in relation to watchkeeping and navigation practices."[50] My safety concerns did not fulfill those expectations but reflected on the operations of BC Ferries and on its use of what I considered substandard and confusing equipment.

. . . .

50 WCAT Decision, 47.

CHAPTER 10

MASTER OF THE SHIP

THE BIG ISSUE WCAT CAME BACK TO TIME AND AGAIN, AND WHICH the BC Ferries officials came back to time and again, concerned the notion of the master's responsibility, the idea that "the responsibilities of a Master (Captain) at sea are akin to that of a 'benevolent dictator.' Captain C spoke of the need for a Master to be compassionate for his crew and to understand the mission but with the knowledge that ultimately 'the buck stops with the Master.' He testified that a Master has no one to turn to but himself and is responsible for all manner of things that take place on his ship, such as (just to name a few) activities in the engineering, catering, or deck departments and issues of passenger service and safety."[1]

This line of reasoning strikes me as particularly ironic in view of the fact that during my nineteen years with BC Ferries, I was consistently in disagreement with the corporation over this very issue of the authority of the master. I took a strong position that the master should be the person in charge of the ship, but with each passing year that seemed to be less the case. In fact, there was a saying in ferry circles that the master "had all of the responsibility but none of the authority." I found maintaining an effective degree of authority over my ship's operation an uphill battle all the way as shore managers and policy makers took ever more authority unto themselves.

I had no say whatsoever in the kinds of ships that BC Ferries built or

. . . .

1   WCAT Decision, 22.

purchased. No say in what modifications would be made or what sort of equipment would be fitted. I had no say in who would be hired, promoted, or fired, or who would be assigned where. In his WCAT testimony Capacci indicated that it "entered his mind" that I should have considered removing Briker from her deck assignment but decided that it would not "have been reasonably possible for the worker [that is, the master] to have made that change in the crew assignment."[2] Consider the contradiction: BC Ferries masters must take responsibility for everything that happens, yet the company acknowledges it might not be "reasonably possible" for a contemporary captain to change a crew assignment.

I fully accepted the master's responsibility. I have never shirked it or denied it. Not before, not during, and not after the accident. But as for authority, I couldn't get even minor safety issues on my ship attended to—if I'd had such sweeping powers, I would not have had that long list of safety problems, many unresolved, that I was obliged to hand over to the Divisional Inquiry.

The *Canada Shipping Act* in force when the *Queen of the North* sank defined the "master" as the person "having command or charge of a vessel." The *Criminal Code* says, "The master or officer in command of a vessel on a voyage is justified in using as much force as he believes, on reasonable grounds, is necessary for the purpose of maintaining good order and discipline on the vessel" (RS, c. C-34, s. 44).[3] That's okay if you're bigger than everyone else and not outnumbered. In practice, a ship's master working for BC Ferries has to rely on his wits. The *Canada Shipping Act* also required

. . . .

2   WCAT Decision, 67.

3   The *Canada Shipping Act* that was in force at the time of the sinking has since been replaced by the *Canada Shipping Act, 2001* (http://laws-lois.justice.gc.ca/eng /acts/c-10.15/20051005/P1TT3xt3.html). Royal Assent to the new act was granted in 2001, but it did not "enter into force" until July 1, 2007. The new act gives the master the right to use "as much force as the master believes on reasonable grounds is necessary for the purpose of maintaining good order and discipline on the vessel" (section 83 (3)). However, *Queen of the North* operated under the old act (http://laws-lois.justice.gc.ca /eng/acts/s-9/20051212/P1TT3xt3.html) and under different regulations. This fact is important to any study of the accident. The version of the Criminal Code in force at the time of the sinking can be found online on the Department of Justice Laws website (http://laws-lois.justice.gc.ca/eng/acts/c-46/20060102/P1TT3xt3.html).

that in all ships over 50 tons net, masters were to sign an agreement with every seaman engaged as part of the crew. Besides information about each seaman, their wages, the ship, and the voyage, this "agreement with the crew" included "any regulations respecting conduct on board, fines, short allowance of provisions or other lawful punishment for misconduct" (RS, 1985, c. S-9, s. 165.2(i)). Since masters traditionally had direct control over every seaman's pay—and every crew member is, under the law, a seaman—the punishments typically involved fines that the master could levy summarily. BC Ferries crew, as employees of the government, were not considered seamen and did not have to sign such an agreement; therefore, I found there was no effective system of ship-board discipline.

When I was with the federal government (in the Coast Guard from 1976 to 1983 and with Department of Fisheries sporadically between 1987 and 1989), punishment was dictated by the *Government Ships Discipline Act* (RSC 1927), which included penalties for infractions of discipline that ranged well into the realm of harshness. When I was a master in the Canadian Coast Guard, we had a policy that spelled out in a table the levels of disciplinary authority for every supervisor for all of the various misdemeanours and offences. For example, a mate could suspend an employee for up to three days for disobeying an order, a master could suspend for up to a week for the same offence, and the level of power increased with one's ranking within the hierarchy. (This has since been replaced by a system of fines.) No such system or equivalent existed at BC Ferries when I was there. I found the master's authority to be more theoretical than actual.

However, when it came time to justify my firing, BC Ferries went to great lengths to portray the modern ferry boat master as wielding authority undiminished from the days of yore when ships had brigs and a cat-o-nine-tails. The most extreme form of this thinking is the hoary old notion that "the captain must go down with the ship." Capacci testified "that it is a maritime tradition that having lost a vessel, the Master of such a vessel would be 'looking to move on' to another place of employment in the maritime world. He indicated that it would be his expectation if he were in that situation. Captain C said that if he had captained a ship that sunk he would expect to be relieved of his command and he 'would move inland with an oar over [his] shoulder.'"[4]

....

4   WCAT Decision, 24.

The WCAT bought into this fine old myth, ruling:

> We find that according to the ethos and principles of
> marine command, as evidenced in the *Canada Shipping
> Act*, the employer's Fleet Regulations, and the testimony
> earlier referred to of Captains C and T, the simple fact that
> the worker was the Master on duty of a ship that sunk
> made him responsible and accountable for the sinking
> of that ship. This is not a matter of blame in the way a
> layperson understands the word, namely, a reference to
> personal fault for specific acts of wrongdoing. Rather, it
> is a statement reflecting the terrible burden of a Master's
> command within the culture of the mariner's world.[5]

The simplest way to deal with the claim that maritime culture or tradition requires captains of ships involved in serious incidents to be fired is
to look at some actual maritime history.

After the *Queen Mary* collided with HMS *Curacao*, cutting her in half
and killing 338 men, her master, Captain Illingworth was promoted by
his company and knighted by King George VI, despite the Admiralty
Court's assignment of blame to both parties. Captain John Boutwood of
the *Curacao* was decorated (Distinguished Service Order).

When Captain Illingworth's successor, Captain G.E. Cove, went
aground with the *Queen Mary* in Cherbourg, he, too, was promoted and
was given command of RMS *Queen Elizabeth*.

The greatest marine disaster in Canadian history was the sinking
of RMS *Empress of Ireland*, in which 1,012 lives were lost, including 840
passengers (more passengers than were lost when the *Titanic* sank). The
master, Captain Henry Kendall, survived. His company, Canadian Pacific,
promoted him. He went on to serve with the Royal Navy through World
War I, achieving the rank of commodore.

The worst peacetime naval disaster in the United States occurred on
September 8, 1923, when nine destroyers of a fourteen-ship formation
ran aground at Point Honda on the California coast. Twenty-three men
were killed. Seven of the ships were total losses. All the captains were

. . . .

5   WCAT Decision, 24.

court-martialled, but the only punishment meted out was to one Captain Edward H. Watson and his navigation officer, Lieutenant-Commander Hunter. Watson, commander of the fleet, who was on the bridge and personally made the navigation error, admitted his full responsibility. His punishment amounted to no more than a loss of promotion points. He continued for another six years as assistant commandant of the US Navy's vast Fourteenth District, headquartered in Hawaii. The other captains were all acquitted.

Moving closer to home, when the Union Steamships passenger vessel *Cheslakee* sank, drowning seven, at Vananda in 1913, Captain John Cockle was in command. The marine court of inquiry found that "the seamanship exhibited by the master and pilot at the time of the disaster was commendable and was the means of avoiding what might have been a much more serious and lamentable catastrophe."[6] Captain Cockle continued with Union Steamships until the outbreak of World War I, when he was welcomed into the service of the British Admiralty.

Some BC captains survived multiple sinkings. On August 15, 1901, the Canadian Pacific steamer *Islander* was holed and sank after leaving Skagway for Vancouver, drowning forty-two. Captain Edmund Charles Le Blank, who had been in command, continued in charge of local ships and was in command of the venerable survey ship and lighthouse tender *Quadra* when she sank in a collision with the passenger vessel *Charmer* in 1916.[7]

The worst tragedy involving a BC coastal steamer occurred on October 24, 1918, when the Canadian Pacific passenger steamer *Princess Sophia* struck Vanderbilt Reef in Lynn Canal with the loss of all 343 aboard. Although Captain L.P. Locke was in command and made a controversial decision not to lower lifeboats, thinking the ship was secure on the reef, the official inquiry attached no blame to him.[8]

Another notable sinking of a passenger vessel in local waters was that of the Gulf Lines' 174-ton *Gulf Stream*, which struck Dinner Rock near Powell River on October 11, 1947, with the loss of five lives. Some

· · · · · · · · · · · ·

6   Gerald Rushton, *Whistle Up the Inlet* (Vancouver: Douglas and McIntyre, 1978), 69.

7   Norman R. Hacking and W. Kaye Lamb, *The Princess Story* (Vancouver: Mitchell Press, 1974), 246.

8   Ibid., 248.

have compared this incident to the grounding of the *Queen of the North*, because both ships struck a prominent feature on a scheduled run amid rumours of irregular crew behaviour. The coroner's jury was "not convinced that proper discipline was maintained" and reported that "definite evidence has been produced to show that members of the ship's company were drinking alcoholic liquids in association with passengers, contrary to what the jury understands to be the ship's standing orders." The officer on watch, second mate Raymond Ketchum, said he "could not explain the deviation in course that would appear to have been made." Captain Jack Craddock, who was in the stateroom of a female passenger when the ship grounded, received a six-month suspension but returned and not only commanded vessels on the BC coast, but also served as a coast pilot supervising other masters.[9]

The alleged "tradition" does not exist even in BC Ferries. There have been numerous serious accidents involving groundings of ferries and collisions, and numerous other accidents including many with loss of life, namely:

- *Chinook II*—Grounded on Snake Island on April 5, 1962. Ship had sailed without a serviceable radar. Master was on the bridge at the time.
- *Queen of Prince Rupert*—Grounded on Haddington Reef on August 11, 1967. Master was on the bridge at the time.
- *Queen of Victoria*—Collided with the Soviet cargo ship *Sergey Yesenin* in Active Pass on August 2, 1970. Three people killed. Daylight, good visibility. The master was on the bridge at the time and had the conduct of the ship. The *Queen of Victoria* was found by the court to be 40 percent to blame. The Supreme Court of Canada found the "wrongful acts or defaults" of the master of the *Queen of Victoria* caused "serious damage to ships and loss of life," but the court did not cancel or suspend his certificate.[10] The master was suspended by BC Ferries but not fired.
- *Queen of Alberni*—Grounded on Collinson Reef in Active Pass on August 9, 1979. Daylight, good visibility. The master was on the bridge

· · · · · · · · · · · ·

9   Articles in *The Coast News* (Gibson's Landing), November 7, 14, 1947.
10   Pollock v. Minister of Transport, [1974] S.C.R. 749, http://scc-csc.lexum.com/scc -csc/scc-csc/en/item/5214/index.do

at the time. The *Tri-City Herald* (Kennewick, Washington) reported on September 13, 1979, that "an investigation has found that an error in judgment by the Master of the British Columbia Ferries' 'Queen of Alberni' caused the ferry to run aground." The investigators "ruled that [the master] had committed 'an error of judgement' (the mildest form of rebuke) and he was quickly reinstated by BC Ferries to full command."[11]

- *Queen of Prince Rupert*—Grounded in Gunboat Pass on August 25, 1982. Daylight, good visibility. The master was on the bridge at the time and had the conduct of the ship. He was demoted to first mate; later offered promotion to master (he declined).
- *Queen of Cowichan*—Collided with a pleasure boat near Horseshoe Bay on August 12, 1985. Three people killed. Daylight, good visibility. The master was on the bridge at the time. The owner of the pleasure craft sued the BC Ferry Corporation, the captain, and the second officer. All were defended by the same legal team (P.D. Lowry and M.A. Clemens). The Supreme Court of British Columbia apportioned two-thirds blame to the *Queen of Cowichan*.[12]
- *Mill Bay*—Grounded at Mill Bay on May 29, 1989. Daylight, good visibility. The captain was alone on the bridge at the time and fell asleep. Demoted *temporarily* to second mate, large vessel.
- *Queen of Saanich*—Collided with the *Royal Vancouver*, a privately owned high-speed catamaran passenger ferry, in the eastern approach to Active Pass on February 6, 1992, injuring twenty-three passengers and crew. The master was on the bridge at the time and had the conduct of the ship.[13]
- *Queen of Alberni*—Collided with a massive bulk carrier *Shinwa Maru*

· · · · · · · · · · · ·

11   Gary Bannerman, *The Ships of British Columbia* (Surrey, BC: Hancock House Publishing, 1985), 102–4.

12   Kwok v. British Columbia Ferry Corp., [1987] B.C.J. No. 2500, Vancouver Registry No. C855199, 20 B.C.L.R. (2d) 318, available from the Laxton Gibbens website, http://www.laxtongibbens.com/personalinjury.html

13   Transportation Safety Board, "Collision between the Canadian ferries 'QUEEN OF SAANICH' and 'ROYAL VANCOUVER,' Northern entrance to Active Pass, British Columbia 06 February 1992," Marine Investigation Report M92W1012 (http://www.tsb.gc.ca/eng/rapports-reports/Marine/1992/m92w1012/m92w1012.asp).

near Tsawwassen on March 12, 1992. Eighteen people were taken to hospital. The master was on the bridge at the time and had the conduct of the ship.

- *Queen of New Westminster*—A vehicle with passengers fell from the upper deck ramp into the water when the ship departed while loading was still going on at Departure Bay on August 13, 1992. Three people were killed: a mother and her two daughters. The master was on the bridge at the time and had the conduct of the ship. After his eventual retirement, the master continued to sail on a contract basis as a master for BC Ferries. The second mate, in charge of loading the upper car deck, was fast-tracked to the position of senior master.

- *Mayne Queen*—Collided with several boats at the marina in Snug Cove and ran aground on November 7, 1995. One vessel was sunk and the *Mayne Queen* suffered damage. The master was on the bridge at the time and had the conduct of the ship. For leaving the scene, the master was demoted from master, minor vessel, to chief officer, large vessel.

- *Queen of Capilano*—Grounded on a rock off Bowyer Island, losing a propeller blade. Daylight, good visibility. The master returned to work and was later promoted to exempt master, major vessel.

- *Mayne Queen*—Grounded off Piers Island on August 12, 1996. Daylight, good visibility. The master was on the bridge at the time and had the conduct of the ship.

- *Spirit of Vancouver Island*—Collided with the power boat *Star Ruby* on September 14, 2000. Two people killed. The master was on the bridge at the time and had the conduct of the ship. (It was the second collision for this master.) Daylight, good visibility. Not fired, continued to command a major vessel.

- *Queen of Surrey*—Collided with the tug *Charles H. Cates V* on January 11, 2004. "Extensive damage" to the tug.[14] Daylight, good visibility. The master was on the bridge at the time and had the conduct of the ship.

- *Queen of Oak Bay*—Collided with twenty-eight small craft—sinking

· · · · · · · · · · · ·

14   Transportation Safety Board, "Collision between the Roll-on/Roll-off Vehicle/ Passenger Ferry *Queen of Surrey* and Assist Tug *Charles H. Cates V,* Horseshoe Bay Terminal, British Columbia, 11 January 2004," Marine Investigation Report M04W0006 (http://www.tsb.gc.ca/eng/rapports-reports/marine/2004/m04w0006/m04w0006 .asp).

some and causing extensive damage to the marina—and ran aground in Horseshoe Bay on June 30, 2005. BC Ferries and its insurers paid out $3 million as a result. Daylight, good visibility. The master was on the bridge at the time and had the conduct of the ship.

Except where I've noted above, I am not aware that any of the masters suffered disciplinary action, and many were promoted.

When George Capacci was the general manager of the Alaska Marine Highway System (Alaska State Ferries), one of his ships, the MV *Kennicott*, ran aground in Wrangell Narrows on June 3, 2003. The master was on the bridge and had the conduct of the vessel. He ordered a turn in the wrong direction and put the ship aground. The accident was caused directly by the actions of the master. The US Coast Guard found that he was negligent and suspended his licence for a term. When asked by the *Juneau Empire* if there would be disciplinary action, Capacci said: "I have every confidence in the world in Capt. ——— and his abilities. I think the public is served by his presence on the ships."[15]

In 1970, a grounding very similar to the *Queen of the North's* involved the Alaska State Ferries' ship *Taku*, which failed to make a planned course alteration and, in clear weather, ran straight into the Kinahan Islands, reportedly at a speed of 17 knots, close to the speed the *Queen of the North* grounded at. Fortunately, the *Taku* struck the islands on a shoaling beach and was damaged but not lost. She was refloated with assistance from, among others, the *Queen of Prince Rupert*, the tanker *Imperial Nanaimo*, the tugs *Rivtow Lion* and *Rivtow Rogue*, along with the smaller tugs *Glendevon* and *Haro*. The first mate and second mate were charged but not the captain; charges against the first mate were later dropped.

After the sinking of the *Queen of the North*, BC Ferries hired Pace Group, a public relations firm, to help it deal with the accident. On its website, the firm notes that, as a result of its efforts, "BC Ferries continued to be viewed as an organization with a deep commitment to safety and an exemplary overall safety record."[16] And George Morfitt noted, in his 2011

· · · · · · · · · · · · ·

15   Masha Herbst, "Ferry Skipper Suspended for Grounding," *Juneau Empire*, July 1, 2003, http://juneauempire.com/stories/070103/loc_ferrygrounding.shtml

16   "Our Work. BC Ferries: Sinking of 'Queen of the North,'" Pace Group website, http://www.pacegroup.com/portfolio-items/bc-ferries-sinking-of-queen-of-the-north

follow-up to the "2007 Report on Operational Safety at British Columbia Ferry Services":

> The 2011/12 corporate business plan sets out the BC Ferries mission: "to provide safe, reliable and efficient marine transportation services which consistently exceed the expectations of our customers, employees and communities, while creating enterprise value." There are five key business plan goals, with the first being the safety objective "to protect our customers and employees by continuously improving the safety of our operations, inclusive of vessels, terminals, and facilities". A number of safety strategies and tactics are listed, along with the statement that "at BC Ferries, the safety of our customers and employees is our top priority."[17]

BC Ferries has had a major incident that is known to the public roughly every two years. There have been eleven deaths between 1970 and 2013. Leaving the dock when a car is driving aboard is hardly exemplary (*Queen of New Westminster*). Neither is running over a pleasure craft while overtaking it in a narrow channel (*Star Ruby*). As for striving to maintain continuous improvement, there have been several major incidents since the sinking of the *North*. Here are a few:

- *Quinsam*—Left the dock while a pickup truck was driving on board in January 2007. The truck fell into the water with the driver narrowly escaping. Daylight, good visibility. The master was on the bridge at the time and had the conduct of the ship.
- *Queen of Nanaimo*—Hard landing at Mayne Island in August 2010, injuring four passengers and two crew members. One of the four injured passengers sued BC Ferries, claiming that her head injury caused her to give up her medical practice.
- *Coastal Inspiration*—Hard landing at Duke Point (struck at a

• • • • • • • • • • •

17   George L. Morfitt, "Safety and BC Ferries: A Follow-up Review of the 2007 Report on Operational Safety at British Columbia Ferry Services Inc.," 22 (www.bcferries.com /files/AboutBCF/Morfitt_Safety_and_BC_Ferries_Report.pdf).

speed of 5 knots with a force of over 12,000 tons/10,880 tonnes) on December 20, 2011. The vessel spent twenty-three days out of service as it underwent repairs. From the TSB report: "There are several ways to control the pitch of both propellers: normal operation, remote emergency pitch control, and local emergency pitch control. There is also an emergency telegraph to provide orders for engine room pitch control using handles, emergency push buttons, or local manual control."[18] The master attempted to use the remote emergency pitch control for the forward propeller. He was not familiar with it so failed to activate its system. As a result, it didn't work. He also failed to take any action with his stern propeller, which was left to continue driving the vessel ahead. The anchors at each end—both manned so that they could be used as brakes in just such an emergency—were never used.

- *Queen of Nanaimo*—Grounded at Village Bay on November 2, 2013. Damage was sustained by the propeller blades, hub, and shaft, and there were indentations made in the hull as well. Additionally, the wing walls that form the dock were damaged.

Again, as far as I know, none of these captains suffered any disciplinary action.

The theory that the captain must always go down with his ship, literally or figuratively, obviously has a lot of flexibility in the way it is applied, even at BC Ferries and even when the captain is on the bridge at the time of the incident. My lawyer, Howard Ehrlich, did his best to counter the company position, and I thought he left no doubt as to the soundness of our case. But the WCAT found in favour of BC Ferries, which reinstated my firing as soon as I brought the *Northern Adventure* back to dock in Port Hardy. Howard and I appealed the decision to the BC Supreme Court and

· · · · · · · · · · · ·

18 Transportation Safety Board, "Striking of Berth, Roll-on/Roll-off Ferry *Coastal Inspiration*, Duke Point, British Columbia, 20 December 2011," Marine Investigation Report M11W0211 (http://www.tsb.gc.ca/eng/rapports-reports/marine/2011/m11w0211/m11w0211.asp).

the BC Court of Appeal, but these courts could only examine matters of law—"Indeed," as Madam Justice Ross wrote in her decision, "it must be emphasized that it is not the function of this Court, on judicial review, to *reweigh* the evidence that was before WCAT."[19] Both courts accepted the facts as presented by WCAT and concerned themselves with legal arguments, none of which came out in my favour.

I was headed inland with an oar over my shoulder whether I wanted to be or not.

19   Henthorne v. British Columbia Ferry Services Inc., 2011 BCSC 409, http://www .canlii.org/en/bc/bcsc/doc/2011/2011bcsc409/2011bcsc409.html

CHAPTER 11

MISSED OPPORTUNITY

WHEN THE BRITISH EXPEDITIONARY FORCE WAS DRIVEN OFF THE continent of Europe in May 1940, the defeat was undeniable, but Britain, led by Winston Churchill, barely broke step. In fact, the British took full advantage of the momentum of their own retreat and turned it around. Fully recognizing the defeat and the inadequacy of their effort, they also recognized, fully, the triumph of the evacuation. Britain regrouped, re-equipped, retrained, and, when they were ready, went back and did it right.

When Edward Dahlgren, Jason Bowman, and I gathered on the bridge of the rescue ship *Sir Wilfrid Laurier*, that is just what we were planning. The triumph of the evacuation would be our rallying point, but every failure would be recognized, and never again would our voices be hushed, never again would our concerns be trivialized. We were not going to take any more bullshit.

Not many people have survived the sinking of a ship at sea. Few survivors of sinking ships have been evacuated with no outside assistance. Very few ship's captains have led such an evacuation. The position I was in, the opportunity we had, was extremely rare. The Transportation Safety Board recognized this:

> In a rapidly developing emergency situation ... masters
> have to rely on their experience and their perception
> of the emergency to make decisions and deal with the
> situation. Given that such experience is rare and given
> that people respond to emergencies in different ways, a

comprehensive evacuation plan is paramount to better prepare the crew for emergencies in the interest of passenger, crew, and vessel safety.[1]

In spite of this insight, the rare individual who has such experience is excluded from evacuation planning.

THE NEW BC FERRIES

Although BC Ferries had been established in 1960, a new act of incorporation in 2003 brought a new management and a new philosophy. A new logo, replacing the familiar dogwood emblem (a dogwood flower on a green background),[2] emphasized that this was ostensibly a new company. In the words of the BC Ferry Commission:

> As a Crown corporation, BC Ferries was very much dependent upon government for everything from rate-setting to vessel construction and spending priorities. Capital investments were approved within the short-term rotation of government fiscal priorities rather than adhering to a long-term business model that is required for a service of this magnitude. In addition, each decision was directly influenced by the politics of the day.
>
> This problem, which has been well chronicled in independent reports about the ferry system, seriously inhibited the corporation's ability to operate in a businesslike manner. With a major capital replacement program needed to upgrade or replace older vessels in the fleet and improve terminal infrastructure, a new model was required to access outside financing to make these necessary investments.[3]

• • • • • • • • • • • •

1   TSB Report, 47.

2   The dogwood is the provincial flower of British Columbia.

3   BC Ferry Commission, "2003: Status Change," in the "FAQs: About BC Ferries" section of BC Ferries Commissioner website, 2014, http://www.bcferrycommission.ca/faqs/about-bc-ferries/from-2003-onwards/

The new structure was a private corporation with a single voting share held by the BC Ferry Authority, "an independent, no-share capital corporation created under the *Coastal Ferry Act* (British Columbia)," which appoints BC Ferries' board of directors and sets the compensation plans for the directors and certain executives. "Both the Authority and BC Ferries operate independently of the provincial government."[4]

When the new management took over, they toured the fleet, delivering a sort of "infomercial" for this new company. We were all pretty cynical. But after meeting with George Capacci when he offered me an excluded position, I came away convinced that it really was a new company with a completely new outlook.

It was Trafford Taylor who alluded to the significance of dropping the old dogwood emblem. I took his words to mean that the dogwood represented the old company and everything associated with it. The new logo represented a fresh start, an attitude of not keeping something just because it's been around a long time. Nothing was sacred. Bad habits and bad ideas all had to go. Too many of them had been kept in the name of tradition. I believed that the old company and all its old baggage was now gone or, at least, going. All the mismanagement of the old company, every defect in design, every shortcoming in training, equipment, and organization was on the chopping block. A revolution in shipping was dawning.

When the *Queen of the North* sank, almost everything that was in it was carried to the bottom. Except for the clothes I wore and the contents of my pockets, all the personal belongings I had on board went down with the ship. Amongst that gear was a bright red T-shirt with the old dogwood crest on it. It had been presented to me by the Safety Department as a token of appreciation for a suggestion I had made. The suggestion was never implemented: too expensive, they said. To me, that shirt symbolized everything that was wrong with the old BC Ferries. Now that the shirt was buried at sea, it symbolized for me the final end of the old company and the dawn of a new and great company.

Based on this belief, Dahlgren and I planned a future of change.

Boy were we naïve.

When Trafford Taylor asked me, at the Divisional Inquiry, why I wished to continue working for BC Ferries, I said that, at the risk of

. . . .

4   From the BC Ferry Authority website, http://www.bcferryauthority.com/

sounding corny, there was symbolism in the things that were buried with the ship, like my dogwood T-shirt.[5] The DI panel completely missed the point.[6] Worse, it seemed to me that management had forgotten their own message about all the ways in which the new company was going to be different from the old.

Had I been invited to help BC Ferries rebuild after the *Queen of the North* sank, here's what I would have recommended.

THE ROLE OF THE MASTER

After the *Titanic* sank in 1912, the first International Convention for Safety of Life at Sea (SOLAS) was passed. In countless discussions and forums since then, a huge amount of ink has been spilled in the name of preventing loss of life at sea. Much finger-pointing, blaming, and derision has also taken place. Many writers have expressed the view that the *Titanic* tragedy was not all in vain, that valuable lessons were learned, and many preventative measures were put in place. Yet ships continue to operate with a highly compromised level of safety. Many of the lessons learned and measures implemented have fallen by the wayside. The SOLAS Convention itself is not applied universally. Prior to the acquisition of the *Northern Adventure*, no vessel in the BC Ferries fleet was classed as a "Convention Ship."[7] This meant an entire set of safety standards was simply not applied.

Looking over the history of shipping and its ongoing safety issues,

. . . .

5   WCAT Decision, 44.

6   According to the WCAT Decision, "Next, we turn to Captain T's question to the worker at the end of the worker's second DI interview. Captain T commented that the worker was not happy and immediately asked him if he still wanted to work for the employer. As we earlier indicated, the DI panel notes are unclear as to the worker's response—Captain C's notes indicate that he said yes but other notes refer to a comment about a shirt with company sayings at the bottom of the sea. Captain T indicated that while he remembered the latter response from the worker at the DI interview, he did not understand what it meant at the time and he still did not know what it means" (57–58).

7   Roxanne Gregory, "B.C. Ferries' Evacuation Systems Come under Fire," *Georgia Straight*, April 23, 2014, http://www.straight.com/news/632216/bc-ferries-evacuation -systems-come-under-fire

campaigning for change seems more than a little discouraging. New, "tougher" regulations are being written all the time, but a plethora of exemptions, waivers, and "compliance plans" reduce the effectiveness of these regulations and produce a false sense of safety.

Shipping companies all over the world, including BC Ferries, talk a lot about the International Safety Management Code—developed by the IMO in the wake of the capsizing of the British passenger ferry *Herald of Free Enterprise*, and adopted by SOLAS in 1994—but they obviously forget what the code says about the master's authority:

> The Assembly adopted resolution A.443(XI), by which it invited all Governments to take the necessary steps to safeguard the shipmaster in the proper discharge of his responsibilities with regard to maritime safety and the protection of the marine environment.

and:

> 5.2 The Company should ensure that the safety management system operating on board the ship contains a clear statement emphasizing the master's authority.[8]

A ship's master is in charge of the *whole* ship. It is absolutely paramount that we root out anything that states or implies anything else. With more than thirty-four years' experience as a ship's master, I can state without reservation that my biggest difficulties come from the constant undermining of the master's authority. Maintaining one's authority is one of the first rules of leadership.[9] In my opinion, it is the weakening of the master's authority that is at the heart of so many of the shipboard problems at BC Ferries.

No modification or alteration of any kind should be made to any ship without the express approval of the master. Every modification or alteration should also be reported in detail to the first mate.

· · · · · · · · · · · ·

8 International Safety Management Code, available on the IMO website, http://www.imo.org/en/OurWork/HumanElement/SafetyManagement/Pages/ISMCode.aspx

9 Len Deighton, *Blood, Tears, and Folly: An Objective Look at World War II* (London: Jonathan Cape, 1993), 301, quoting Field Marshal Erwin Rommel.

BRIDGE RESOURCE MANAGEMENT

When I returned to BC Ferries as master of the *Northern Adventure*, I was told, several times, "There have been a lot of changes; I think you're going to like it."

There were improvements, but in general I was disappointed with the changes. The problem was that debatable assumptions had been made, and the numerous changes were based on those assumptions.

One example was the blanket assumption that a lack of Bridge Resource Management training must have been a factor in the accident. In my opinion it was not a factor, but the DI's recommendations included "Bridge Resource Management (BRM) training should be provided to all personnel who work as deck officers," and "development of a Bridge Resource Management (BRM) training course for unlicenced bridge personnel" was also to be investigated.[10] In the months following the sinking, Prince Rupert–based crews were sent for BRM training. Contrary to the expectations, their instructor observed that they were "the best team we ever had here; you do exactly what you're supposed to do."

Bridge Resource Management is an imitation of aviation's Crew Resource Management (CRM), originally Cockpit Resource Management. In the 1970s, a number of professionals in aviation began to express their concerns about the role of human factors in aviation accidents. Informal observations led to formal studies concerning those human factors, which were identified as a wide range of knowledge, skills, and attitudes, including communications, situational awareness, problem solving, decision making, and teamwork. Each of these has its own subdisciplines. For example, leadership is a subdiscipline of teamwork.

There is nothing new about any of this. All of these elements have been around since before man learned to walk upright. What was new was the formal recognition of such elements, and the new importance that came to be placed on them both during training and during everyday operations.

At a 1979 workshop "Resource Management on the Flightdeck," sponsored by the National Aeronautics and Space Administration (NASA), the concept of "cockpit resource management" was introduced as "a method

· · · · · · · · · · ·

10 Divisional Inquiry, 26.

of training crews" to make "better use of the human resources on the flight-deck."[11] In 1986, NASA held another workshop that led to the integration of CRM into all aspects of training and expanded its scope beyond the cockpit to become *Crew* Resource Management, encompassing the entire crew as well as dispatchers, air traffic controllers, and maintenance personnel. The American Federal Aviation Administration now defines CRM as "the effective use of all resources: human resources, hardware, and information."

The maritime world caught on to the idea in the 1990s and made an attempt at adapting the airline industry's training to ships. BRM training seems to have begun in 1993.[12] By 2003 it also underwent a subtle but important change in concept (not yet adopted by all) when the Swedish Club began offering courses in "maritime resource management," which it defined as "the use and co-ordination of all the skills, knowledge, experience and resources available to the team to achieve the established goals of safety and efficiency of a voyage or any other safety critical task." The main reason behind the name change was to remove the restriction of the bridge and include engineers, pilots, and relevant shore-based staff at ship management companies—all of whom influence safety at sea.

Canada is among the countries that have lagged behind these developments and continue with BRM, a term whose definition *limits* the resources that should be available—the very opposite of the goal. A ship's master and mates are not constrained to the bridge in any way resembling how pilots are confined to the cockpit. Resource management in a ship is much more encompassing. It needs to include the entire *unified* crew, the whole ship, and the resources outside the ship. Unfortunately, BRM got started

· · · · · · · · · · · ·

11   G.E. Cooper, M.D. White, and J.K. Lauber, *Resource Management on the Flightdeck: Proceedings of a NASA/Industry Workshop*, NASA Conference Publication No. CP-2120 (Moffett Field, CA: NASA—Ames Research Center, 1980); Robert L. Helmreich, Ashleigh C. Merritt, and John A. Wilhelm, "The Evolution of Crew Resource Management Training in Commercial Aviation," *International Journal of Aviation Psychology* 9, no. 1 (1999): 19–32, DOI: 10.1207/s15327108ijap0901_2.

12   Martin Hernqvist, manager of Maritime Resource Management for the Swedish Club (a marine insurance company), "Brief Information on the Maritime Resource Management (MRM) Training Course," October 2007, http://www.intertanko.com /Topics/Marine-safety/Marine-safety-/The-Maritime-Resource-Management-MRM -training-course/

without an understanding of the underlying philosophy of CRM, which is that pilots should never restrict their available resources unnecessarily.

Most BRM courses include some examination and discussion of case histories. The first course I took included a report of a ship navigating a river in the United States. Approaching a bridge that crossed the river at a bend, the pilot realized the engine had shut down. As a result, and despite his efforts to steer and to stop forward movement by dropping the anchor, the ship struck the bridge, carried on to strike two vessels lying alongside a quay, ploughed through the quay, and demolished several occupied buildings. The cause of the loss of propulsion was the action of the engineer who, noticing that the oil pressure had fallen to 10 pounds per square inch (68.9 kilopascals), reacted by shutting off the engine. Putting the value of engine bearings above all else, he caused huge damage and endangered human life. Had he acted appropriately by informing the pilot and leaving decisions to the people in charge, this accident would have been averted, and the engine would probably not have sustained any damage.

In its analysis, the US National Transportation Safety Board (NTSB) made no mention of the engineer's action as the direct cause of the accident; nor did the board mention his lack of communication or the folly of building such a ship with only one engine and no effective warning systems. They also did not mention that a contributing factor to this very costly accident was the decision to build a road bridge at a bend in the river. The NTSB offered no suggestions for how the collision could have been avoided but instead blamed it on poor BRM and criticized the bridge team and the way they communicated. The real cause—a bad decision by an unauthorized person—received no attention. In fact, the NTSB criticized the engineer only for his poor English, which he didn't use anyway. Our instructor agreed with the report. Obviously, such an approach to accident analysis can never lead to the appropriate corrective actions.

This and other misconceptions put forward in BRM courses result in a negative value. If it were properly conceived and all-encompassing, BRM would be a great thing. But to achieve this, a few things must be recognized. One of these is an awareness of human fallibility, including one's own fallibility. An ideal BRM program would teach all of us to recognize fallibility in ourselves and in others. Ed Haynes, the captain of United Airlines Flight 232, which crashed in Sioux City, Iowa, on July 19, 1989, gives a good example of this when he says:

Up until 1980, we kind of worked on the concept that the captain was THE authority on the aircraft. What he said, goes. And we lost a few airplanes because of that. Sometimes the captain isn't as smart as we thought he was. And we would listen to him, and do what he said, and we wouldn't know what he's talking about. And we had 103 years of flying experience there in the cockpit [of Flight 232], trying to get that airplane on the ground, not one minute of which we had actually practiced, any one of us. So why would I know more about getting that airplane on the ground under those conditions than the other three. So if I hadn't used [CRM], if we had not let everybody put their input in, it's a cinch we wouldn't have made it.[13]

Another concept crucial to CRM is the ability to win an argument with one's superior. I don't mean just the ability to present an argument; I mean the ability to win it. The crash of Air Ontario Flight 1363 on March 10, 1989, was a major impetus to the development and adoption of CRM and is invariably referred to in CRM courses and in discussions. Flight 1363, a Fokker F-28, crashed on takeoff due to an excessive accumulation of ice and snow on the wings. Twenty-four of the sixty-nine passengers died. The two cabin attendants, as well as off-duty pilots who were travelling on the plane, were aware of the danger caused by ice and snow on the wings, but did not bring this to the pilot's attention or question his decision to take off—the attendants felt they would have been dismissed by the pilot, and the off-duty pilots felt it wasn't their place to interfere, so, again, there was a reluctance to challenge a person in authority. According to CRM, all these "resources" should have given their input when they felt the plane was in danger.[14]

• • • • • • • • • • • •

13 Al Haynes, "The Crash of United Flight 232," presentation at NASA Ames Research Center/Dryden Flight Research Facility, Edwards, CA, May 24, 1991, http://yarchive.net /air/airliners/dc10_sioux_city.html

14 The commission of inquiry into the accident was led by Mr. Justice V.P. Moshansky; see the next section.

THE HUMAN FACTORS

After Air Ontario Flight 1363 crashed in 1989, Justice Virgil P. Moshansky was commissioned to head an inquiry into the accident. His landmark report, the result of three years of research and interviews, sets a high standard for accident investigations.[15] Moshansky examined what he referred to as "the entire aviation system," and because he understood the importance of human factors in such an accident, Moshansky supplemented the expertise of his Canadian team with two internationally recognized experts in human factors. One was Dr. Robert Heimreich, who was involved in the selection of astronauts for NASA's space program; the other was David Adams, deputy director of the Australian Bureau of Air Safety Investigation. Moshansky understood that he had the opportunity to make a significant contribution to aviation safety. He took the approach that "the discovery of human error is only the starting part of the investigation."[16] As one commentator noted, "The immediate reaction [in the case of the Dryden crash] was that a pilot error was responsible. In hindsight, there were obvious threats which it appeared the pilot recklessly disregarded. However, this view drastically oversimplified the situation the pilot faced. The actual accident investigation went deeper and found that organizational factors and specific circumstances placed the pilot in a goal conflict and double bind (note the report needed four volumes to lay out all of the different organizational factors and how they created the latent conditions for this accident)."[17]

In the case of the *Queen of the North*, investigators discovered only that an error of some kind had to have been made. They never discovered what that error actually was, or whether there was more than one error.

. . . .

15 Virgil P. Moshansky, *Commission of Inquiry into the Air Ontario Crash at Dryden, Ontario: Final Report*, 3 vol. (Ottawa: Minister of Supply and Services Canada, 1972).

16 Address by Mr. Justice V.P. Moshansky to the Annual Conference of the Alberta Aviation Council, Lake Louise, October 10, 1992, reported in *Canadian Aviation News*, 1992.

17 David D. Woods and Richard I. Cook, "Perspectives on Human Error: Hindsight Biases and Local Rationality," available on the National Interagency Fire Center website, http://www.nifc.gov/index.html

By not knowing what error was made, they had no chance of discovering how or why the error was made and, therefore, they came nowhere near the discovery of the cause and how a similar accident could be prevented in future.

To discover and then go on to understand the faulty decisions of a man with over 10,000 hours of navigational experience, a man of good character and conscience, whose competency was certified by the Minister of Transport, whose proficiency was vetted by the officers of a large and well-established coastal fleet, requires a look well beyond the obvious and more than a cursory and generic look at the human factor. The TSB report on the *Queen of the North* contained only one sentence that explained a human factor, and a footnote reference to an authoritative work.

TRAINING AND TESTING

I am alive today because I had a crew that could have launched the lifeboats and life rafts with their eyes closed. I don't think that could be said of many of today's crews—not because of any deficiency on their part, but because the equipment they have been saddled with cannot be exercised on a regular basis.

Regarding equipment-specific training, the Morfitt Report had this to say: "We also noted the views of deck officers with respect to familiarization with navigation equipment. Generally, we found no consensus within this group about the extent of training and orientation when new bridge and navigational equipment is installed. Some interviewees indicated that training for bridge navigation equipment is 'excellent,' with deck officers required to sign off for clearance. Others believed the company could improve the process of preparing crews to operate new equipment and suggested they be prepared at refit or sent to vendor orientations."[18]

. . . .

18   George Morfitt, "Safety and BC Ferries: A Review of Operational Safety at British Columbia Ferries Services Inc." (January 2007), 50. Under the heading "Review Procedures," Morfitt states: "This review was conducted over a period of five months by me and contracted professional staff under my direction. The services of a consulting firm with recognized expertise in marine safety management, were also retained" (5).

As I noted in Chapter 7, the practice of having masters and mates sign for their own competency is just plain crazy. The correct procedure would be to have comprehensive training provided, followed by an adequate quiz, followed by a discussion and clarification of any parts shown to be unclear in the mind of the trainee. Only when the instructor is satisfied would the clearance be signed *by the instructor.*

The industry needs to take an aviation approach to training. The training must encompass the limitations, capabilities, and pertinent technical knowledge of the equipment and the techniques. Training situations must be realistic and include such problems as lost radar targets, unexpected failures of equipment, and dealing with belligerent traffic. Radar simulator training needs to be one-on-one. Training in navigation is not just about operating equipment. Navigation is a skill and should be taught as such.

Among the major impediments to training are the widespread misconceptions about it. Training can include drills, but the routine drills conducted by ship's crews are not training. They are simply regular exercises for people who are already trained.

The simple act of providing information should also not be confused with training. Ship-specific and route-specific familiarization, similarly, is not training; it is provided to fully trained personnel who are joining a specific class of ship or a route for the first time. In my mind, the word "training" should be reserved for ordered practical instruction and exercise. It should not include classroom time or study time—those activities are separate and supplementary to training. Time spent accruing sea time is an ordeal and a necessary experience-gathering process, but it is not training.

Testing needs to be practical as well as written and oral.

DESIGN

Critics often cite "human error," "operator error," or "pilot error" as the prime contributory cause of an accident. Never do they cite "designer error," "engineer error," or "nerd error."

I am not clowning when I say "nerd error." The term "nerd" was coined by Theodor Seuss Geisel, known better by his pen name, Dr. Seuss. A nerd, according to popular usage, lacks language skill, social skill, and practicality.[19] Nerds are viewed with affection by modern society due to their tremendous contributions to computer sciences and programming. But society overlooks the danger in leaving design decisions to a group of people for whom clear communication is not always paramount.

In its report on Asiana Flight 214, which crashed on landing in San Francisco after striking a seawall on July 6, 2013, the US NTSB made numerous findings, including "mismanagement" of the flight by the pilots, "nonstandard communication and coordination between the pilot flying and the pilot monitoring," "flight crew fatigue which likely degraded their performance," and a need for enhanced training. It also reported "the need for … reduced design complexity of the airplane's autoflight system."[20]

Chris Hart, acting chairman of the NTSB, put it this way: "In their efforts to compensate for the unreliability of human performance, the designers of automated control systems have unwittingly created opportunities for new error types that can be even more serious than those they were seeking to avoid."[21]

Recommendations of this sort are not found in the TSB report on the grounding of the *Queen of the North*, nor have I found them in any other marine accident reports that I have read. But there are three automated systems that I would propose banning from all ships: improper propulsion system default positions, automatic shut-off switches for engines, and ill-conceived navigation alarms.

· · · · · · · · · · · ·

19 As defined by *Merriam-Webster's Collegiate Dictionary*, 11th Edition, "a creature in the children's book *If I Ran the Zoo* (1950) by Dr. Seuss … ; an unstylish, unattractive, or socially inept person; esp: one slavishly devoted to intellectual or academic pursuits."

20 NTSB, "Board Meeting: Crash of Asiana Flight 214 Accident Report Summary," June 24, 2014, http://www.ntsb.gov/news/events/Pages/2014_Asiana_BMG-Abstract.aspx

21 Quoted in Adam Withnall, "Asiana Airlines Flight 214 Crash Caused by Boeing Planes Being 'Overly Complicated,'" Independent (UK), June 25, 2014, http://www.independent.co.uk/news/world/americas/asiana-airlines-flight-214-crash-caused-by-boeing-planes-being-overly-complicated-9562331.html

DEFAULT POSITION

ASSOCIATED PRESS March 5, 2010. Toyota's "black box" information is emerging as a critical legal issue amid the recall of 8 million vehicles by the world's largest automaker. The National Highway Transportation Safety Administration said this week that 52 people have died in crashes linked to accelerator problems, triggering an avalanche of lawsuits.

REUTERS June 3, 2014. Reuter reported on Tuesday that an analysis of statistics held in the Fatality Analysis Reporting System (FARS) national database of crash information reveals that 74 car accident deaths between the years 2003 and 2010 occurred in GM cars with since-recalled ignition switches, and are typical of the incidents previously reported by the automaker.

GM recalled 2.4 million vehicles over the past several months after it was discovered that a problem with their ignition switch caused cars to shut off while driving, disabling power steering, anti-lock brakes and airbags.

When these cases arose, no car owner that I ever heard of accepted the outcry of indignant corporate executives and engineers who claimed that a sudden engine failure or a gas pedal stuck in the "floored" position were safety features. Owners demanded a solution and the manufacturers were forced to act. Yet ships all around the world have equivalent features built in and rationalized with exactly the same claim. Most of the ships in the BC Ferries fleet have engines that will shut down with no warning and a propulsion system that, just like Toyota's gas pedal, defaults to the "full ahead" position. The designers and the "experts" say that automatic kill switches are absolutely necessary for the good of the engine, and the full-ahead default is "the get-home capability." Why do the owners go along with it? Because, unlike the case of most automobiles, a ship is owned by one group of people and operated by another.

In August 2010, the *Queen of Nanaimo* slammed into the wing walls of her dock while attempting to dock at Village Bay. BC Ferries later revealed that two steel dowels in the oil distribution box had become loose and fallen out. When the essential parts dropped out of the system, the propeller pitch moved to its default position: "full ahead." Six people were injured (four passengers and two crew). BC Ferries and the ship's master were sued. The lawsuit claimed that the plaintiff, a medical doctor, had suffered a serious head injury which "caused permanent disabilities including pain, loss of memory and concentration, depression, headaches, and sleep disturbance. She now needs help to manage her affairs, has had to receive nursing care from family members, and has suffered a loss of income."[22]

On November 7, 2013, the passenger ferry *Princess of Acadia*, operated by Bay Ferries between Nova Scotia and New Brunswick, also lost propeller pitch control and, consequently, ran aground at Digby, Nova Scotia. In her case, a modification made ten years earlier had altered the default position to "full astern." The subsequent TSB report noted this but provided no reason for the modification. The report detailed the events—a loss of the main generators, which resulted in loss of electrical power to the controllable pitch propeller (CPP) system, which caused the system to seek its default position of full astern which drove the ship aground.[23] Five months previously, the ship experienced a similar incident but the master was able to avoid disaster by de-clutching the engines in time. (Emergency de-clutching is available on the bridges of only a minority of ships.) The TSB was very critical of the master, the engineers, and the company but made no finding as to the extreme inadvisability of the equipment manufacturer's selecting "full astern" as the default condition.

An almost identical grounding occurred in Warrenpoint Harbour, Northern Ireland, in 2008 when the cargo ship *Moondance* suffered a blackout (electrical power failure), went full astern as a result, and grounded. The accident was investigated by the Bahamas Maritime Authority (the ship was Bahamas registered), which criticized the crew at great length

. . . .

22   Jane Seyd, "West Vancouver Doctor Sues Ferries over Crash," *North Shore News*, August 12, 2012, http://www.nsnews.com/news/west-vancouver-doctor-sues-ferries -over-crash-1.345313

23   Transportation Safety Board, "Grounding, Roll-on/Roll-off Passenger Vessel *Princess of Acadia* Approaching the Digby Ferry Terminal, Digby, Nova Scotia, 07 November 2013," Marine Investigation Report M13M0287 (http://www.tsb.gc.ca/eng /rapports-reports/marine/2013/m13m0287/m13m0287.asp).

over all manner of issues such as poor communications, poor ship knowledge, and "complacent procedures."

Regarding the default position, the report was neutral but at least acknowledged the inherent risks:

> Most CPP systems default to the full astern position when a total hydraulic oil failure occurs while the shaft is rotating. Some systems are designed to default to full ahead, and a lesser number default to the neutral or zero pitch position. It is a matter of opinion as to which is the preferred default position. Each failure mode brings with it its own problems and risk of collision or contact.[24]

Incidents of this type are not rare. The feature of having "full ahead" as the default setting in order to provide a "get home" capability is completely unnecessary as a manual control could easily be provided in all CPP systems. Defaulting to "full astern" makes little sense.

AUTOMATIC ENGINE SHUT-OFF SWITCHES

In its report on the *Queen of the North,* TSB introduced the subject of the *Estonia* disaster in order to illustrate its suggestion that life rafts should be self-inflating so that when a ship sinks, any life rafts remaining aboard would inflate and float free.[25] Although it would have made no difference in our case, I agree with this recommendation. I have a recommendation of my own that is also based on witness testimony from the *Estonia*, which sank on September 28, 1994, while crossing the Baltic Sea from Tallinn, Estonia, to Stockholm, Sweden.

Time and again when reading accounts from the survivors of that

. . . .

24   Marine Accident Investigation Branch, "Report on the Investigation of the Electrical Blackout and Subsequent Grounding of the Ro-Ro Cargo Ship Moondance," Report No 5/2009 (February 2009), 44, https://www.gov.uk/maib-reports/electrical -blackout-and-subsequent-grounding-of-ro-ro-cargo-vessel-moondance-in-warrenpoint -harbour-northern-ireland

25   TSB Report, 43.

sinking, I have noticed that what seems to be certain death is averted in the nick of time simply because of the sudden availability of light—either a flashlight or a momentary restoration of the ship's electrical power. It is reasonable to assume, then, that some of the 852 dead would be alive today if the lights hadn't been deliberately taken away from them when the ship's engines or generators stopped working.

Unlike a modern aircraft engine, which will continue to run even when turned upside down, ship's engines lose oil pressure when inclined more than a few degrees. This is the case both with the main engines (which propel the ship) and the generators (or "auxiliary" engines). Unbelievably, many ships are fitted with automatic switches that immediately turn the engines off when the oil pressure drops below a pre-set limit (usually 10 pounds per square inch/68.9 kilopascals). This is what happened to the people on board the *Estonia*. Passengers and crew who were fighting for their lives—desperately trying to escape, trying to free life rafts, lifeboats, and life jackets—were plunged into darkness so the engines could be preserved and the ship could go to the bottom with her engine bearings in pristine condition. Somewhere an engineer must be smiling.

Numerous groundings have resulted from propulsion failures, including some of the worst environmental disasters. The Shetland grounding of the oil tanker *Braer*, which was a total loss and involved the spillage of 93,700 tons (85,000 tonnes) of crude oil, is a good example of what can happen as the result of a propulsion failure.

Ship's engines and generators should be designed so that oil pressure will not be lost when the ship is inclined at least as far as its angle of vanishing stability (the angle at which a ship has tilted so far that it will not right itself). The *Estonia*'s generators should have been run until they either seized or melted. Automatic shut-off switches of any kind should be banned (along with their proponents).

ALARMS

Many designers seem to have a firm belief in the value of built-in alarms, which appears to stem from their cynical view that the operators of the equipment they design are simply not to be trusted. These alarms would sound constantly for no significant reason if they were allowed to be left activated.

If designers were to consult and work with navigators (the *right* navigators), it would be possible to come up with alarm systems that have a true benefit. Until alarms are designed to be practical, they will be more of a distraction than anything else. The conversation between Lilgert and Briker was only one of the events that the TSB identified as having "interrupted" Lilgert's routine sequence of making a course change. The weather was another. And the ECS alarm was the third. Since that report was issued, many people have said and written a lot about the conversation, a little about the weather, and nothing about the alarm.

EMERGENCY PLANNING

In 1983, I left my job as master of a Canadian Coast Guard cutter and took a job as a second mate with Dome Petroleum (Canadian Marine Drilling, Ltd.), which was involved in oil exploration in the Beaufort Sea. (This is where I got my icebreaking experience.) Dome had two large icebreaking supply ships, *Canmar Kigoriak* and *Robert Lemeur*. I sailed in both. The first mate I sailed with was a man named John McKinnon. John had been assigned the task of drawing up the emergency muster list for fire and boat stations. This is a minimum requirement for every vessel, but John was not the sort of person who would meet only the minimum requirements. His muster lists were comprehensive and very carefully planned.

When that project was complete, he went on to draw up emergency procedures for every contingency—fire and abandoning ship, but also grounding, flooding, engine failures, electrical failures, collision, and man overboard. Each emergency procedure was in checklist form, with everything in proper sequence and no lengthy or awkward wording. Each list was comprehensive.

One of the most important things I ever did as a mariner was make copies of those checklists for myself. For every ship in which I sailed, I produced emergency checklists based on those drawn up by John McKinnon. Over the years I made minor changes to suit specific ships. When the *Queen of the North* grounded, it was the "Grounding" checklist, originally produced by John McKinnon, revised slightly by me, and reproduced in a Plexiglas lamination, that we used. I credit it as one of the chief reasons we escaped with our lives. I owe a great debt to John McKinnon, as I do to all the others who taught and mentored me over the years.

Equipped with a well-developed approach to emergency planning, I instituted the routine and equipment for cabin searches. When I joined the ship, there was no such system or equivalent system in place. I brought in a dedicated key cabinet with master keys for emergency use only, a set of flashlights, and the supply of chalk to be issued to each person doing cabin searches. I also wrote the instructions for carrying out cabin searches (please see Appendix D).

PASSENGER LISTS

In September 2009, three and a half years after the sinking, the northern ships still did not have cabin assignment lists. BC Ferries used the same system as before but did take one additional step. The old system merely recorded the name of the person who reserved the cabin. Cabins were frequently reserved by one person on behalf of another; the person who made the reservation might not be travelling at all. Under the system that came into use after the *Queen of the North* sank, when the cabin was sold on board, the name of the person taking it was recorded and the list was faxed to shore. The cabin could have bunks for two or four, but no names were recorded other than that of the person who paid for it. The solution to this problem is so obvious that readers would be insulted were I to present it.

After the sinking of the *Queen of the North,* the federal Fire and Boat Drills Regulations were amended to make it mandatory for a ship to carry a list of passengers if the voyage was longer than twelve hours, if there was at least one assigned passenger berth, or if it was a Near Coastal Voyage Class 1 (formerly Home Trade Class II). These stipulations would cover both Route 10 (Prince Rupert–Vancouver Island) and Route 11 (Prince Rupert–Skidegate).

One of the emergency preparedness steps I had taken during the years before the sinking was to have permanent, weather-proof roll call lists (rolls) posted at every boat and raft station in both the *Queen of the North* and the *Queen of Prince Rupert.* They were lists of crew rather than names, as the names change regularly but the crew positions do not. I also made sure that the muster list (AKA "watch and quarter bill") appointed one person at each station to be in charge. This made it quick and easy to call roll at any muster. For passengers, however, there was no roll, no list of passenger names.

Another step I took was to equip each station with a grease pencil in a waterproof pouch. The pouches were fastened to the undersides of the life-jacket locker lids. The purpose was to mark the tally of people onto the respective davit as each craft was loaded. Over the years, I frequently discovered that the grease pencils had been removed. On such occasions I would replace them, but on the night of the sinking, none could be found. Counting heads sounds like an easy task, but it is not as easy as it sounds, even under good conditions. The total I had when I left the ship was 102. I knew that the log book said 101. Regardless of the question about the passenger cabin manifest, I knew that the cabins had been searched. To make doubly sure, I made my quick run-through of the cabin areas while eleven anxious crew waited in the starboard lifeboat, watching the ship sink deeper and deeper. When the Coast Guard asked me if I was certain all were safe, my reply was, "Negative." Because we were not certain, an intensive search proceeded.

SAFETY

Only in a very few professions or occupations are the lives of others so dependent on the skills and knowledge of those who have taken on their safety. As Justice Moshansky pointed out,

> any notion of absolute safety is a myth. What is in issue is the maintenance of an acceptable level of safety, or its converse, an acceptable level of risk. An acceptable level of safety is a compromise between the accomplishment of the task at hand and the protection of human life and property from accidental damage or destruction during the accomplishment of that task. The trick in making risk management decisions is to make such decisions based on facts and not simply on value judgments.[26]

What, then, of the slogan "Safety is our first priority"? This is widely

· · · · · · · · · · · ·
26 Address by Mr. Justice V.P. Moshansky to the Annual Conference of the Alberta Aviation Council, Lake Louise, October 10, 1992, reported in *Canadian Aviation News*, 1992.

publicized by all kinds of corporations in all manner of businesses, especially those involved in transportation. "Pernicious and dangerous nonsense" is what J.E.D. Williams calls it: "If we really mean that safety is paramount we would stay home."[27]

Slogans are in abundant supply at many of today's corporations, and I despair that such nonsense has become their stock in trade. "Safety is everyone's responsibility"; "the whole organization [is] responsible for safety"; etc. In *Beyond Aviation Human Factors*, Maurino, Reason, Johnston, and Lee describe that approach as "haphazard" and argue that "such a simplistic view ... denies the technological and sociological realities of contemporary aviation."[28]

The true result of such thinking is that safety has no priority.

Another defensive slogan is that a company or a procedure "meets or exceeds all regulations." In the case of a company like BC Ferries, this raises the question "Which regulations?" Apart from the *Northern Adventure*, its vessels are exempt from the SOLAS Convention and the company is exempt from many other regulations as well, so it may meet and exceed its own regulations, but not those rules created by international bodies that have studied myriad shipwrecks and accidents.

When Edward Dahlgren, Jason Bowman, and I gathered on the bridge of the rescue ship *Sir Wilfrid Laurier* after the sinking of the *Queen of the North* and articulated our vision of a bold new BC Ferries, I imagined a future where I would be fully engaged in implementing lessons we had all gathered from our collective experience, such as those described above. It was not to be, but I hope we are not the last to be seized with the ambition to bring in fresh new approaches.

· · · · · · · · · · · ·

27   J.E.D. Williams. *From Sails to Satellites: The Origin and Development of Navigational Science* (Oxford University Press, 1992), 266–67.

28   Daniel Maurino, James Reason, Neil Johnston, Rob Lee, *Beyond Aviation Human Factors* (Aldershot, UK: Avebury Aviation, 1995), 76.

CHAPTER 12

AFTERMATH

THE WRECK OF THE *QUEEN OF THE NORTH* STILL RESTS AT THE BOT-tom of the ocean, and there are no plans to do anything with it. Shortly after the sinking, David Hahn estimated that to bring the *Queen of the North* to the surface would cost $100 million, and he didn't see value in that.[1] I have never heard of sunken ships being raised from anything deeper than harbour or estuary depths. There are also no plans to recover environmentally damaging contaminants—mainly fuel—from the wreck. The ship is in 1,400 feet (427 metres) of water, and its compartmentalized design would make any fuel recovery operation very complex. Fuel has never been recovered from a ship of this type at this depth anywhere in the world.

It's impossible to know how much fuel is left onboard. When the *Queen of the North* collided with Gil Island, it was carrying 58,000 gallons (220,000 litres) of diesel, 9,700 gallons (36,600 litres) of engine lubricating oils, about 264 gallons (1,000 litres) of gasoline (in vehicles), and an estimated 37 gallons (140 litres) of other fluid contaminants. Diesel tanks may have ruptured on impact with Gil Island or the seafloor, and diesel would have also escaped through vent pipes as the ship sank. No one knows what happened to the engine lubricating oil—some of it would have been in the engine and may not have leaked immediately—or the other fluid

. . . .

1   Scott Deveau, "BC Ferries Slapped with Suit over Sinking," *Globe and Mail*, March 28, 2006, http://www.theglobeandmail.com/news/national/bc-ferries-slapped-with -suit-over-sinking/article23004151/

contaminants. According to a BC Ferries press release of April 5, 2006, "A Unified Command Incident Command Post, consisting of BC Ferries, Ministry of Environment and Environment Canada representatives, has been established in Prince Rupert to respond to the environmental impacts of the Queen of the North sinking … Burrard Clean Operations (BCO), under contract to BC Ferries, is leading the containment activities at the incident site using 6,050 feet of barrier boom to protect sensitive areas," and "Hartley Bay and Kitkatla First Nations representatives have provided valuable input regarding sensitive sites and boom placements. In addition, eight Hartley Bay residents have been trained to use boom equipment to assist BCO, if necessary."[2]

Fortunately, the environmental damage at the time did not seem to be severe. Diesel fuel evaporates quickly, and most of the spilled oil disappeared within a few days. Andre Breault of the Canadian Wildlife Service estimated hundreds of birds had been exposed to oil, but no birds had been found dead. At some of the strands in the vicinity, mussels, cockles, clams, and other intertidal life were contaminated with oil, but the detectable concentrations of oil rapidly declined in the months following the accident. Shellfish harvesting usually ends in March and doesn't start up again until around October. No health advisories were issued.[3]

However, although the initial spill has mostly evaporated or been cleaned up, new fuel occasionally wells up from the wreck. A year and a half after the sinking, the average leakage rate was determined to be 0.11 gallons (0.4 litres) per day, and five years after the sinking the ship was still releasing small amounts of fuel. From 2006 to 2011, BC Ferries, through its insurance company, paid the Gitga'at Development Corporation, which oversees land use, tourism, fisheries, and economic development for the Hartley Bay Indian Band, to monitor the wreck site.

• • • • • • • • • • • •

2   "Summary #3—Queen of the North," BC Ferries Quick Facts, press release, April 5, 2006, retrieved from http://www3.telus.net/Tsawwassen/Queen%20of%20the%20North.htm (September 11, 2015).

3   John Harper, Doug Bright, and Mike Sanborn, "*Queen of the North* Monitoring: Summary Review," report from Coastal & Ocean Resources, Inc., April 11, 2007, http://foi.bcferries.com/2012-030-responsiverecords6.pdf

BC Ferries' insurer also paid for shellfish bed monitoring for two years in exchange for the results of shellfish analysis. In 2011, BC Ferries' insurance company decided there was "no tangible benefit to continuing daily upwelling monitoring" and discontinued funding.[4] The Hartley Bay Band Council protested that its agreement was with BC Ferries, not the insurance company, and wrote to the BC Ferry Commission, asking that the company "do what is morally and ethically correct, and do its part to minimize all potential risk to the environment of the largest remaining intact coastal temperate rainforest in the world." In the meantime, the band pays for the monitoring that it feels "has been thrown on them by an insurer whom they have never met and never had any obligation or agreement with."[5]

Not satisfied with BC Ferries' decision to leave the ship alone, the Hartley Bay Indian Band had filed a lawsuit against BC Ferries in 2008 for damages to fisheries. In 2011 the band again called for the ship to be raised. Chief Councillor Bob Hill says there is evidence to show that at least half of the fuel is still onboard, and he claims that David Hahn initially promised that all the contaminants would be removed by late 2006.[6] Hill and other residents of Hartley Bay say that there are no safeguards against a sudden upwelling of diesel fuel.

LAWSUITS

A week after the sinking, passengers Maria and Alexander Kotai launched a lawsuit against BC Ferries. The couple had been moving to Nanaimo, and most of their valuables, including their car, family photos, and heirlooms, went down with the ship. The Kotais sued BC Ferries for negligence and

. . . .

4   "Queen of the North Monitoring Summary," BC Ferries press release, May 6, 2011, http://foi.bcferries.com/2012-030-monitoringsummary.pdf

5   Letter from Hartley Bay Band Council to Gordon Macatee, Commissionaire, BC Ferry Commission, June 11, 2011, http://www.bcferrycommission.ca/wp-content /uploads/2012/01/Hartley-Bay-Band-Council-11-06-11.pdf

6   "BC Ferries Nearing Decision on Queen of the North Fuel Cleanup," Canada.com, April 22, 2007.

asked for compensation for their belongings (valued at $98,000), and for pain and suffering.[7] Their lawyer got the case certified as class action, arguing that all the passengers on the ship went through a common experience. Under the *Marine Liability Act*, the owner's liability does not depend on proof of fault or negligence. In other words, they are liable unless they can prove that they were not negligent or otherwise at fault. Because the lawyers wanted to prove "recklessness" on our part and get more money, they came after me, Lilgert, and Briker, as well.

The class action suit was settled in 2010. In the end it represented forty-four passengers, and Lilgert, Briker, and I were removed as defendants. The total value of the settlement was $354,600, but two-thirds of that went to pay legal costs, so the amount to be divided between passengers was just over $141,000. Brandice Seabrook, who suffered from anxiety every time she saw the BC Ferries logo, received $35,000, the largest amount paid to a single person. Maria and Alexander Kotai each received $10,000. Makenna Harding, who was nine at the time of the sinking, received $2,500. She was diagnosed with post-traumatic stress disorder and suffered from night terrors and anxiety. Twenty of the passengers who were upset by the experience but weren't able to prove a recognizable psychiatric illness received $500 each.[8] Many passengers were unhappy with their compensation, but, according to their lawyer, "The general sentiment has been to put this behind them, whether or not the settlement lives up to their expectations, which obviously it doesn't," so no one filed an appeal.[9]

Some passengers launched independent suits against BC Ferries. Gerald Foisy's daughters, Brittni and Morgan, sought damages for wrongful death but didn't have the money to go to trial. They eventually settled out of court and received $200,000, less lawyer's fees, for loss of love, guidance, affection, financial support, and inheritance from their father. Brittni

· · · · · · · · · · ·

7   "Ferry-Sinking Lawsuit Not Class Action: Lawyer," Canadian Press, June 12, 2007, http://www.ctvnews.ca/ferry-sinking-lawsuit-not-class-action-lawyer-1.244620

8   Kotai v. Queen of the North (Ship), 2010 BCSC 1180 (CanLII), http://www.canlii .org/en/bc/bcsc/doc/2010/2010bcsc1180/2010bcsc1180.html

9   James Keller, "Survivors of BC Ferries Sinking Settle Suit," *Globe and Mail*, July 22, 2010, http://www.theglobeandmail.com/news/british-columbia/survivors-of-bc -ferries-sinking-settle-suit/article564838/

received $69,509.90; Morgan, who is three years younger, $75,538.70.[10] Brent and Brandon Rosette also sued and settled. Their settlement terms have never been made public.

BC Ferries received $67.9 million in insurance. The company kept $6.6 million to pay for future insurable losses, and the rest was used to pay for passenger claims, environmental cleanup, and part of the cost of a replacement ship. The new ship cost $99.1 million including modifications, and another $3.7 million in terminal upgrades.[11]

THE *QUEEN*'S REPLACEMENT

The *Northern Adventure* (originally the *Sonia*), the ship that replaced the *Queen of the North*, had been built in Greece and was purchased by BC Ferries in September 2006, even though Jerzy Trzesicki and Peter Estabrooks, two senior Transport Canada marine inspectors who inspected the ship, found it was in "poor condition ... despite the fact the vessel had valid certificates and was only two years old ... There were signs of poor electrical maintenance, fire hazards, and no supplementary emergency lighting system to be found."[12] They were also concerned that, in the event of an emergency, the ship might not meet the evacuation requirements.

The company reportedly spent $50.6 million to buy the ship and some $50 million more on taxes and travel to British Columbia, and work in Greece and at Victoria Shipyards.[13] Then there was a rush to get the ship ready for service by March 31, 2007. This deadline was met, but an investigative journalist in Victoria later discovered that the ship sailed

• • • • • • • • • • • •

10   Anupreet Sandhu Bhamra, "Ferry Sinking Case Settled," *Globe and Mail*, August 21, 2009, http://www.theglobeandmail.com/news/national/ferry-sinking-case-settled /article1388214/

11   British Columbia Ferry Services Inc. and BC Ferry Authority, *Annual Report 2006/07* (Victoria: Author, 2007), 9, 33, 36, 46–47.

12   Andrew MacLeod, "BC Ferries Rushed Ship into Service Despite Safety Worries," *The Tyee*, September 19, 2011, http://thetyee.ca/News/2011/09/19/BCFerries_Slip_Ship/

13   Andrew MacLeod, "'Northern Adventure' Wasn't Safe to Sail: Union Inspector," *The Tyee*, March 11, 2009, http://thetyee.ca/News/2009/03/11/Adventure/

with a temporary certificate and a list of deficiencies that would have to be corrected: there were not enough lifejackets for passengers and crew, a lifeboat-lowering device was not working, and the elevator and escalator were locked until they could be inspected. As well, it appeared that it sailed without "an evacuation analysis," even though this requirement "would seem particularly significant given that the company was replacing a vessel that had sunk on the same route the Northern Adventure would be serving."[14]

There was a three-hour delay before the ship's first voyage from Port Hardy to Prince Rupert on March 31, 2007, and a thirty-hour delay before a sailing a week later.

Captain David Badior, president of the ships' officers component of the Ferry Workers' Union, sailed on the ferry in mid-April and wrote a scathing report of the *Northern Adventure*'s condition. He "made a 'by no means exhaustive' list of 17 things he observed himself," including the fact that the ship's "ARPA, which uses radar to track a vessel's position in relation to other ships or land, was not working"; the lifeboats were "literally locked and chained into their cradles and not allowed to be used"; there were "stickers all over the place for fire equipment that is not there"; "the ship had no stand-alone general alarm, nor a public address system"; and there was "no apparent documentation on anything, no vessel specific manuals, no equipment specific manuals nothing. As an example on the rescue boat davit in plain view for the passengers to see is a felt pen note saying that no one knows what the accumulator pressure is supposed to be so keep it charged at 60 bar and the Nitrogen bottle at 80 bar until they can get documentation."

Badior also commented that "many of the crew members looked exhausted but were still working their darnedest to make the ship work. I was told numerous times that the vessel was a lot better yesterday (the 20th) than when they first sailed her three or so weeks ago. All this and the Crew are now working a split shift supposedly to make things safer when in fact they are getting 4.5 to 6 hours of sleep a day if they are lucky. I won't get into the many stories about intimidation by Management."

He concluded, "I am stunned that anyone in Operations accepted the

. . . .
14   MacLeod, "BC Ferries Rushed Ship into Service."

Northern Adventure in the condition she is in today let alone what it was like aboard a couple of weeks ago."

"What exactly did B.C. Ferries learn from the Queen of the North's sinking?" Badior asked rhetorically. "Nothing!"[15]

The *Northern Adventure* is still on the northern route, joined by the *Northern Expedition* in 2009. The *Queen of Prince Rupert* was retired when the *Northern Expedition* arrived.

CREW AND CAPTAIN

In December 2008, the Justice Institute of British Columbia recognized the crew of the *Queen of the North* with a Heroes and Rescuers award. The award was in the form of an engraved ship's bell on a mahogany mounting. BC Ferries president David Hahn received the award at a dinner. BC Ferries did not tell me of this award; nor, to my knowledge, did it inform any of the crew who earned it at such great personal cost. Apparently Hahn accepted it on our behalf and took it back to head office. I only became aware of the award because someone happened to see a tiny article about it in the back pages of a newspaper.

Unable to endure life in Prince Rupert, Karl Lilgert sold the Dodge Cove home he had built and bought an orchard in Grand Forks. On March 17, 2010, the RCMP arrested him and charged him with two counts of criminal negligence causing death, which carries a maximum penalty of life imprisonment. His trial was held from January to May 2013, and the jury convicted him. He appealed the verdict, but the BC Court of Appeal upheld the conviction and the Supreme Court of Canada denied further appeals. He began serving his four-year sentence in December 2014.[16]

Of the forty-two who manned the ship that night, BC Ferries fired five and demoted one. Fourteen were badly traumatized and could never go

. . . .

15   MacLeod, "'Northern Adventure' Wasn't Safe to Sail."

16   Canadian Press, "Supreme Court Says It Won't Hear Appeal in Deadly B.C. Ferry Sinking," *Globe and Mail*, May 14, 2015, http://www.theglobeandmail.com/news /british-columbia/supreme-court-says-it-wont-hear-appeal-in-deadly-bc-ferry-sinking /article24433995/

back to sea (some were unable even to go on board a ship, and one was unable to go to the beach)—nine of them were forced to quit and five retired early. Two of the crew transferred to day ships so they would never have to sleep on board again. Nineteen continued to sail in the Northern Service. One was promoted.

Lynn Cloutier's escape from her flooded cabin left her with chronic pain syndrome and post-traumatic stress disorder. She never worked again. She fought for nine years before she won her case for compensation. Going into "retirement," she continues to endure the injuries that robbed her of her working life and deprive her of the kind of life that should have been hers.

It took me more than six years to recover my career after being fired, and the recovery is not a full one. In the years immediately after I was fired, I exhausted all the available opportunities in my profession and ended up looking for unskilled jobs outside of it. I was fortunate and extremely grateful to gain part-time work aboard an inland ferry running between Galena Bay and Shelter Bay on Upper Arrow Lake. Captain Elgin McKillop hired me for that job, and I am indebted to him, as I am to the company. (The president of the company, Western Pacific Marine, was Graham Clarke who, as a passenger, survived the sinking of the *Queen of the North*.)

I was hired as a first mate but not full time. In an effort to make ends meet, I also had to accept work as a deckhand when it was available. So, at the age of fifty-six, thirty-five years after I took my first command, and when I should have been thinking about retirement, I swept, scrubbed, and mopped decks; cleaned toilets; shovelled snow; and chipped ice. Some days were healing, others not so much. To my shipmates who accepted me, I will always be grateful.

After a time, I was able to acquire some additional work as first mate on the Kootenay Lake ferry running between Balfour and Kootenay Bay.

I now have an interesting, challenging job as a rescue co-ordinator with the Canadian Coast Guard. Rescue co-ordinators work at an extremely high professional level, but the monetary reward is drastically reduced from what I had been making as a captain in the Northern Service of BC Ferries. My expenses are also higher now, and I have yet to make up the ground lost during those six-plus years of searching.

There have been other challenges since 2006. From the time I arrived at the Crest Hotel in Prince Rupert directly following the sinking, I was surprised that I seemed to be not at all traumatized. I had no symptoms of post-traumatic stress disorder. None, that is, until around half-past midnight every blasted night, when I would become wide awake and unable to go back to sleep. I didn't wake up frightened or trembling or sweating. I just woke up and couldn't get to sleep again.

To compensate, I started going to bed at a ridiculously early hour. Trouble was, any time there was a sudden noise, my heart would jolt, my stomach would jolt, and the butterflies in my stomach would remain in full flight as my heart pounded. As soon as I sat up, no problem—it all went away, and no noise, no matter how sudden and no matter how loud, would bother me in the least. I could go around all day and not be bothered, whether by memories or by any sudden noises, but as soon as I lay down, a sudden noise always had the same jolting effect.

I remember one night in particular. I had gone to bed very early. My wife was in the kitchen putting away the dishes, and as each plate was placed in the cupboard, my heart and stomach did their mad jumps. Even though I knew there was another one coming, the same thing happened every time I heard that little "click." I would say to myself, "Look. You're at home. You're safe. Stop this nonsense." But it did no good. When I sat up, the responses stopped. But as soon as I lay down, they would start up again.

It was my chiropractor, Dr. Gordon Hasick, who put me on the right track. He told me about a treatment called Eye Movement De-sensitization and Re-processing (EMDR). When we experience a trauma, the old saying that the heart sees things before the mind is actually true. The body is the first one on scene, then the emotions, then the mind. Once the emergency has passed, the brain will re-process it; we will "sleep on it," talk about it, think about it, and, after a while, the emotions are done and we only have a memory of it all. Sometimes, though, the right brain remains closed off—in lock-down. EMDR works by opening up the communication link between right and left brain so that the re-processing can take place.

The results of my treatment were immediate, and with each visit I was less and less affected by sudden noises. After six or seven visits I was sleeping through the night, and I have not had to go back.

In the days and weeks that followed the sinking, I received a flood of cards and letters from supporters and well-wishers. They came from colleagues, shipmates, friends, family, and strangers. People I had not seen since high school wrote or phoned to wish me well, make sure I was all right, and give their support. Some wrote letters to the editor and called up radio talk shows in my support. I am grateful to them all. To this day I meet people—professional mariners and non-mariners—who compliment me when they learn who I am.

The sinking of my ship spelled the end of many things and the beginning of new things, but, above all, a continuation of life. For many who have escaped death, there is the feeling that we have been handed a second chance, almost a second life with the past life still existent. The past does not go away, the list of regrets gets no shorter, but there is a kind of redemption or, at least, the opportunity for one. I have found that the vividness of the past makes the present that much more vivid. When I look at the beautiful world around me I feel fantastic. Joyful.

I won't forget the sinking of the *Queen of the North*. What I can do is choose how I respond to the memories and realities and the feelings that come with them. The feelings that are hardest to control are about those who went through that midnight hour with me on March 22, 2006, those whose lives were changed forever along with mine. To them I offer this thought that has been of help to me: the night of the sinking does not define us; it is only a part of who and what we are.

EXTRACT FROM THE CODE OF BUSINESS CONDUCT AND ETHICS, BRITISH COLUMBIA FERRY SERVICES

"If an employee has concerns about safety issues, he or she must report them immediately to his or her Manager or, alternatively, through the Company's safety management systems."

—From the BC Ferries website

MY LETTER TO THE VILLAGE OF HARTLEY BAY

June 4, 2006

Patricia Sterritt
Chief Councillor
Hartley Bay
V0V 1A0

Dear Chief Councillor,

Please forgive me for being so long before thanking the people of Hartley Bay for their quick, selfless, and expert assistance to us when we were forced to abandon the *Queen of the North*. I had originally planned to visit and thank all of you in person; unfortunately, the ongoing investigation puts me in a position where I am extremely restricted in the contact I can make.

I was the captain that night and I can say everything done by your village and her boats was superb. If someone was to write a textbook on how a coastal community should respond to a marine distress, Hartley Bay would have to be the basis for it.

Please pass on to all the village my sincere thanks.

For superb seamanship, for quick and clear thinking, and for the will to help, my hat is off to the people of Hartley Bay.

Yours truly,
Captain Colin Henthorne

KARL LILGERT'S APOLOGY STATEMENT

To everyone that was impacted by the sinking of the *Queen of the North*.

I regret [that] this tragic accident occurred and its impact on all involved.

I continue to grieve for the missing persons and would with all my heart exchange my life for theirs.

I am sorry for the children of the missing persons and their families.

I am sorry for the passengers who survived, for their trauma and loss.

I am sorry for my shipmates for having to go through this tragic traumatic accident, who did everything they could.

I am sorry for all involved that still to this day are having difficulty because of this traumatic accident.

I am sorry to BC Ferry and Marine Workers' Union for the grief and financial strain this disaster has created. I feel humble and indebted for the unconditional support I have received from them.

I am sorry for BC Ferries for having to deal with this tragedy.

I am sorry for my family and friends that were impacted by this tragic accident. I am grateful for your understanding and support.

I am thankful for the community of Hartley Bay who opened their community and assisted the rescue.

Words are inadequate for the sorrow and grief I feel. There isn't a day that goes by that I don't think about everyone that was impacted by this tragic accident. For all of this I am deeply sorry.

Sincerely,
Karl Lilgert

EXAMPLE OF PASSENGER CONTROL DUTIES

PASSENGER CONTROL

The purpose of Passenger Control is to save lives. In the event of an emergency, Passenger Control will:

1. Direct Passengers to Safety.
2. Control panic.
3. Search cabins.
4. Assist passengers with donning lifejackets.
5. Prevent passengers from returning to cleared areas.

These things are much easier said than done, however, they can be accomplished through good, clear, calm, and assertive communication. Directing passengers "to Safety" could mean directing them to Boat and Raft Stations, or to a designated Assembly Area in the ship which is removed from danger.

The Chief Steward co-ordinates all Passenger Control in liaison with Command. Good communication—between the Passenger Control Crew and the Chief Steward—and between the Chief Steward and Command—is of paramount importance.

In a fire emergency, Crew designated to Passenger Control may also be required to close the fire dampers in their respective areas and provide boundary cooling.

EDN ____ CATERING - DECK #___ STARBOARD SIDE AFT[1]

Report to the Purser's Office.
Pick up:

1. Emergency keys.
2. Chalk.
3. Flashlight.

Proceed to **Deck ___ Starboard Side.**

SEARCH CABINS AND CLOSE ALL FIRE DAMPERS IN THIS AREA.

Open each cabin door on the starboard side and *search* the cabin to make *sure* it is vacant. Remember to look under the beds and in bathrooms. People will do odd things in an emergency. Frightened children and even adults will sometimes hide.

Instruct the passengers to put on warm clothing and direct them to the declared Assembly Area (if one has been declared) or the Boat and Raft Stations as ordered.

Once you have made sure that the cabin is empty, **lock** the cabin door and mark it with a large *X* to indicate that it has been searched.

Proceed to the next cabin. When all your cabins have been searched and evacuated, cordon off that area.

*EDNS ___, ___, and ___ work as a team to clear all the cabins on the starboard side of this deck. If you finish your cabins first, you continue to check other cabins on this deck until they are all done. The report is made to the Purser's Square when all the cabins on the starboard side have been checked.

Report to the Chief Steward:

"DECK ___ STARBOARD SIDE: ALL PASSENGER CABINS ARE CLEAR."

. . . .

1   Each employee has an Employee Designator Number. In this case, the duties described below are for a person in the Catering Department, whose station is on the right-hand side of the ship toward the stern.

Continue with your other emergency duties as instructed, *i.e.,* muster at the Assembly Area, Boat and Raft Stations, or Fire Station.

COMMUNICATIONS: If, for some reason, it is necessary to communicate but you are unable to leave the zone, each cabin has a phone line to the Purser's Office. Know how to use it but remember that the Purser's Office might be very busy and not able to answer right away.

CHRONOLOGY

March 22, 2006. Times are in Pacific Standard Time using the twenty-four-hour clock.

0021 The *Queen of the North* strikes ground.[1]

0022 Ship's initial call to Prince Rupert Traffic: "*We have run aground.*"

0026 Ship's call to Prince Rupert Radio: "*We require assistance immediately.*"

0033 Prince Rupert Radio alerts the Joint Rescue Co-ordination Centre (JRCC).

0053 The master and the last of the crew abandons ship. [This time is also from the TSB Report.]

0056 Fishing vessel on scene reports the *Queen of the North* "abandoned." The fishing vessels *April Augusta* and *Lone Star* circle the ship and report they do not see anyone on board.

· · · · · · · · · · · ·

1   Time is taken from the TSB Report, which took the time from the ship's ECS computer, so it should be accurate. All other times in the Chronology are taken from the Incident Log at JRCC.

0139   JRCC receives the report relayed from the *Lone Star* that the *Queen of the North* has sunk.

0159   Fast Response Craft (FRC) from the Canadian Coast Guard Ship *Sir Wilfrid Laurier* arrives on scene.

0210   The *Sir Wilfrid Laurier* arrives on scene.

0305   Prince Rupert Coast Guard Radio reports forty-seven people from the ship are in Hartley Bay and the fishing boat *Lone Star* has seventeen more headed for Hartley Bay.

0327   The *Sir Wilfrid Laurier* confirms they have thirty-eight survivors from the *Queen of the North*, and there are sixty-four in Hartley Bay for a total of 102.

0338   Mona Danes (relaying communications from Hartley Bay) advises JRCC that their head count is sixty-four.

0343   The *Sir Wilfrid Laurier* recounts: confirms thirty-seven, making a total of 101 people recovered.

0352   Prince Rupert Coast Guard Radio advises JRCC that the last count from Hartley Bay is sixty-five.

0536   The *Sir Wilfrid Laurier* sends Seaman Briker, Fourth Mate Lilgert, Second Mate Hilton, and First Mate St. Pierre and five passengers from Hartley Bay to Prince Rupert by helicopter.

0728   JRCC faxes a list of all survivors on board the *Sir Wilfrid Laurier* (a total of thirty-six) to BC Ferries Vice-President Capacci at BC Ferries Head Office.

0822   Prince Rupert Coast Guard Radio advises that Coast Guard Helicopter 356 is airborne from Seal Cove (Prince Rupert) with three people on board: pilot, pollution officer, and BC Ferries rep.

0833   Capacci advises JRCC that they have reconciled all lists and he is convinced that there were only ninety-nine people on board the *Queen of the North*, forty-two crew and fifty-seven passengers, and all are accounted for; passenger Shane Pearson did not travel and passenger Paul Madsen was counted twice, which accounted for the previous total of **101** believed to have sailed with the ship.

1221   The First Mate of the *Sir Wilfrid Laurier* advises JRCC that he conducted a head count and reviewed the passenger list and also interviewed passengers. He believes that two persons were left behind in Hartley Bay.

SPECIFICATIONS OF THE *QUEEN OF THE NORTH*

Built 1969 at Weser Werk Seebeck, Bremerhaven, Germany

Port of registry Victoria

Official number 368854

Call sign VCQD

Original name *Stena Danica*

Other former name *Queen of Surrey*

Configuration Twin screw, twin rudders, single bowthruster

Length 410 feet (125 metres)

Beam 65 feet (20 metres)

Gross tonnage 8,889 (Lloyd's Register) / 8,807 (Canadian List of Shipping)

Draft 17 feet 3 inches (5.3 metres) (maximum)

Top of mainmast to keel 120 feet 5 inches (36.7 metres)

Top of mainmast to waterline 103 feet 2 inches (31.5 metres) (Summer Load Water Line)

Main engines 2 MAN Type V8V 40/54 V-16 turbo-charged, after-cooled. 7,800 BHP each. Non-reversing, direct-acting.

Bore 15.75 inches (40 centimetres)

Stroke 21.26 inches (54 centimetres)

Power 2 × 7,800 BHP = 15,600 BHP @ 360 RPM

Classification Lloyd's 100A1

Ice class 3

Lloyd's number 6917267

Fuel capacity 476 tons (432 tonnes)

Construction Welded steel, transverse framing system, double bottom

HISTORICAL NOTES

Sister ships to the *Queen of the North* There were no ships identical to the *Queen of the North*, but two very similar ships were the *Stena Germanica* and *Stena Britannica*.

STENA GERMANICA

- built 1967
- sold and renamed *A Regina* 1972
- wrecked 1985

STENA BRITANNICA

- built 1967
- sold and renamed *Wickersham* 1968
- sold and renamed *Viking 6* 1974
- renamed *Goelo* 1980
- renamed *Viking 6* 1982
- sold and renamed *Sol Olympia* 1982
- sold and renamed *Sun Express* 1985
- then renamed *Viking 6*
- scrapped 1985

GLOSSARY

An italicized word in a definition indicates that the word is also defined in this glossary.

abeam   abreast (of the ship)

able seaman   a *seaman* whose experience, knowledge, and abilities are certified. He may steer but not navigate the vessel. The abbreviation is AB, which is often taken to mean "able-bodied seaman"; however, it is merely the first two letters of "able."

aft   toward the *stern*

after   situated toward the *stern*

amidships   see *midships*

Automatic Radar Plotting Aid (ARPA)   a computer attached to the *radar*. When the operator selects a target (an echo on the radar screen that represents an object such as land or another vessel), the ARPA locks on to it ("acquires it") and from then on automatically tracks it. Once the target has been under the ARPA's surveillance for a sufficient length of time, the computer provides a full set of information on the target: its speed, course, and closest point of approach (CPA, the closest distance that the target and the operator's ship will pass). It will also predict the time to go until the CPA is reached. At the same time, it assigns the target a vector, represented by a section of line originating at the target, and lying in the direction in which the target is travelling. The vector's length represents the distance it will travel in the length of time selected by the operator. The vector can be used in a number of ways, for example, the operator can predict whether the other vessel will pass ahead or astern. He can also predict where, geographically, the two vessels will make their CPA.

autopilot (automatic pilot) a system that keeps a ship moving on a desired *heading*; it does not navigate or pilot

bearing a direction as viewed from the ship; the horizontal angle between the reference point on which the bearing is taken and true north is a true bearing; between the reference point and magnetic north is a magnetic bearing; and between the reference point and the ship's head is a relative bearing. If the bearing is taken with a compass that is not corrected for deviation, it is called a compass bearing.

bow the forward end of the ship

bowsing-in tackles *tackles* that hold a lifeboat against the side of a ship so it can be boarded

bridge a raised structure running across or along the ship. In the *Queen of the North* there was only a navigating bridge from which the ship was steered and navigated. Navigation instruments, controls, and communications gear were fitted there.

bulkhead a wall inside a ship

cable 1. originally, a larger rope made by winding three ropes together. Today it is used to mean the anchor chain. 2. One-tenth of a *nautical mile* (0.185 kilometres).

chief engineer the person in charge of the engine room department

chief steward the person in charge of catering and passenger services on board a BC Ferry

chronometric gyro repeater a type of *gyro compass* repeater, so named because of the way the instrument clicks in steps (in the manner of a chronometer) as the dial rotates. The clicks are audible and will betray any unwanted turning or, in their absence, failure to turn. This type of device has prevented many a disaster.

clutter the echoes of rain drops and ocean waves that reflect the *radar* signal and appear on the radar screen. Various electronic devices are used to reduce this clutter.

controllable pitch propeller A ship's propeller is a form of helical screw. Its pitch is the distance that it would advance (ignoring slip) in one revolution; it is determined by the angles of the blades in relation to the hub. Variable pitch means that this angle can be changed by mechanical means. Controllable pitch means that the pitch is directly controlled by the operator. In many ships, including the *Queen of the North,* propeller reversing is achieved by changing the pitch through neutral and into reverse pitch while the propeller continues to revolve in the same direction.

course the direction in which a ship is being steered

course made good the actual direction that a ship has travelled while on a certain *course* (often differs from the intended course due to influence of current, wind, etc.)

crew excluding the *master*, every person employed or engaged in any capacity on board the ship

davit a type of derrick or crane

deck what would be called the "floor" in a house

deck department   the department of the *crew* whose responsibilities include navigation, cargo, and all other aspects except those that fall to the catering and engine room departments

deckhead   what would be called the "ceiling" in a house

dogwood   the provincial flower of British Columbia. From 1960 until 2003 the dogwood was the emblem of BC Ferries, displayed on the house flag and on the ship's funnels.

Doppler speed log   an instrument for measuring a ship's speed. It sends an acoustic signal downward, and this signal echoes off the sea floor or off a layer of colder water and back up to the instrument. The processor calculates the Doppler shift (change in frequency) and converts the information into units of speed (*knots*) and distance travelled (*nautical miles*).

echo sounder   (also called depth sounder) an instrument for measuring the depth of water beneath a ship. It sends an acoustic signal downward, and this signal echoes off the sea floor and back up to the instrument. The processor calculates the time elapsed for the echo to return and converts the information into units of depth (feet, *fathoms*, or metres).

electronic chart system (ECS)   an electronic chart display system that is not approved by IMO (those types which are approved are termed ECDIS); this was the type fitted in the *Queen of the North*. In addition to displaying the chart, it is coupled to an electronic navigation system (usually GPS) and, based on input from that system, displays the position of the ship. It provides information such as the speed made good (AKA speed over the ground) and *course made good*. It can be programmed with a ship's route; when this is done, it can provide expected times of arrival (ETAS), vectors, alerts, and prompts for track monitoring and course alterations. It also records some voyage data, such as positon, *track, heading*, and speed.

excluded employee   one who is not entitled to union membership. The term has been replaced, in some circles, by the more anti-union term "exempt."

fall   the line (rope) used in a *tackle*, winch, derrick, or *davit*

fathom   a unit of measurement equivalent to 6 feet (1.8 metres), part of the decimalized system of measurement used in navigation; it is 1/100th of a *cable* and 1/1000 of a *nautical mile*

ferry   a vessel for transporting people or vehicles across a short stretch, such as a river, lake, harbour, or strait. The proper term for the *Queen of the North* was "car-carrying passenger ship."

first mate   second-in-command of a ship; often misnamed "first officer," "chief officer," or, in broken English, "chief mate." The first *mate* is in direct charge of the *deck department*.

following sea   the condition when the ship is travelling in the same direction as the waves

forecastle   (pronounced fōc śul) a raised *superstructure* at the *bow*. The term includes the *deck* at its top as well as the space and structure below it.

forward   toward the *bow*

frames   the ribs of a ship

freeboard   the part of a ship's side between the *waterline* and the *deck*

gyro compass   a non-magnetic type of mechanical compass that uses a gyroscope (a wheel mounted so that its axis can turn in all directions while maintaining the same absolute direction) and its property of maintaining "rigidity in space" to provide directional information. Multiple remote displays called "repeaters" can be fed from the master gyro and can be conveniently located for the purpose of steering and taking *bearings* both visually and by *radar*. A ship's gyro compass seeks true north, being guided by complex mechanical devices that align it with the earth's axis.

heading   the direction in which a ship is pointing; that is, the direction of her fore-and-aft line

helm   the instrument or device by which a ship or boat is steered

helmsman   the *seaman* who steers the ship (see *quartermaster*)

houseworks, house   structures built separately from the *hull* and *superstructure*. The superstructure extends to the sides of the ship; houseworks do not.

hull   the body of the ship, excluding the *houseworks*

jog steering   a type of steering that uses a short lever in place of a steering wheel for fast-response steering control

keel   the bottom centre-line of the ship; strictly speaking, the lowest and principal structural member in the ship's construction, running lengthwise

knot   one *nautical mile* per hour

list, listing   the condition of a ship when it is inclined to one side or the other is called a *list* when it is caused by internal force, i.e., by a weight that is off the centre-line. When caused by an external force, such as wind, it is called "heel."

log   1. Any instrument that measures the speed of a ship through the water. 2. A record book (log book). Ship's logs record all significant events, particularly *courses*, speeds, and position. My standing orders required the position to be logged at intervals not exceeding twenty minutes.

magnetic compass   a compass that aligns with the magnetic force lines of the earth and points generally at the north magnetic pole. On the BC coast, the difference from true north (the geographical north pole) is in the range of 20 degrees. Magnetic *bearings* and *headings* are those taken in reference to magnetic north.

master   the person in command of the ship; the captain

mate   under the Crewing Regulations (2006), "'mate', in respect of a ship, means a person, other than the *master*, a *pilot* or a *rating*, who has charge of the navigation, manœuvring, operation or security of the ship"

Mayday   the spoken word "Mayday" is an international distress signal

Mayday relay   a Mayday signal repeated by another radio station on behalf of the vessel in distress

midships   also amidships; the middle of the ship; this could mean "on the centre-line" or it could mean "mid length." It is also used to describe the neutral position of the ship's rudder.

nautical mile   a unit of measurement that is part of the decimalized system of measurement used in navigation; it is 100 *cables* and 1,000 *fathoms*. The British Standard Nautical Mile is 6,080 feet (1,853.18 metres); the International Nautical Mile is 6,076.10 feet (1,852 metres).

parallel index   a *radar* navigation technique that is used to maintain a specified *track*. A suitable landmark is selected, and a line parallel to the desired track for the ship is superimposed on the radar screen at the appropriate distance off. It is also used for altering course, for anchorage approaches, for the identification of a radar-inconspicuous object, to establish a clear anchor berth, and to avoid collisions. See figure on page 89.

pilot   a mariner who comes from outside the *crew*, holds a pilot's licence, and takes the conduct of the ship. Pilotage Regulations stipulate the conditions under which pilotage is compulsory.

pitching   the motion of a ship when the *bow* and *stern* rise and fall alternately

port   the left-hand side of the ship (when one is facing forward)

purser   in a commercial ship, the person in charge of the financial side of the administration of the ship's company, particularly the passengers. At BC Ferries there is no such appointment, although the word is still in use in the terms "purser's office" (*steward's* office) and "purser's square" (the *deck* space in front of the purser's office).

quartermaster   a *seaman* who is entrusted with the steering of the vessel. Quartermasters are also entrusted with security duties such as fire and security rounds, gangway watch, etc., and taking soundings.

radar (RAdio Detecting And Ranging)   an instrument that sends out a super-high-frequency radio signal, which is reflected back as echoes by the objects that it hits. The denser the object hit, the stronger the echo (for example, metal returns a stronger echo than plastic or fibreglass). The echoes are converted by the receiver in such a way that they display on a screen, so the radar provides a picture of all radio-reflective objects surrounding the ship. It is used for geographical reference, collision avoidance, and searching. Together with the compass, it is the most important of modern marine navigational instruments.

raster chart   a direct copy or scan of an existing paper chart, presented on an *electronic chart system* or electronic chart display information system

rating   a person who is a member of a ship's *crew* other than an officer

rescue boat   could be any boat used in a rescue, but in BC Ferries it refers to a boat that is carried specifically to rescue a man overboard. It is also referred to as a shepherd boat when used to tow and round up life rafts.

roll-on/roll-off vessel   a vessel on which the cargo comprises wheeled vehicles or is loaded by wheeled vehicles: i.e., the cargo rolls on and rolls off. Car ferries are an example of roll-on/roll-off vessels.

rubbing strake   (also called belting) originally an extra plank fitted around a vessel to provide a buffer when coming alongside another vessel or other object; in modern ships it is fabricated steel, and in the *Queen of the North* it lay even with the car *deck* (it could be said to have been an outer extension of the car deck)

S-band radar   a *radar* that operates on a wavelength of around 3.9 inches (10 centimetres) and a frequency of around 3 GHz. It produces a radar picture that is less detailed and sharp than the *X-band radar* but is much less affected by precipitation and by ocean waves. It is what the navigator turns to when the X-band radar has reached the limit of its effectiveness in heavy rain and/or seas.

seaman   1. any sailor or mariner; 2. under the *Merchant Shipping Act* and the *Canada Shipping Act* (later replaced by the *Canada Shipping Act, 2001*), the term included every person "employed or engaged in any capacity on board any ship." The term is generally used on board ship to mean an ordinary seaman or an *able seaman*. The former has training and skill but not certification. The latter holds a certificate of competency as an able seaman.

starboard   the right-hand side of the ship (when one is facing forward)

stern   the back end of the ship

superstructure   the extension of the *hull* above the *freeboard* deck, which in the *Queen of the North*'s case was the car deck. Above the *freeboard* deck, the ship is not fully watertight. Not to be confused with *housework*, which is structurally separate.

tackle   an arrangement of blocks (pulleys) with a line run through them. On shore it is commonly called "a block and tackle."

tank top   the top of the double bottom, so-called because double bottoms are divided into tanks. These are generally used for carrying water, fuel, oil, ballast, etc., or are left empty for the purpose of buoyancy. The *Queen of the North* carried no fuel or oil in the double bottom tanks.

track   the route that the navigator plans to take

under way   the condition of a ship that is not at anchor, made fast to the shore, or aground

vector charts   electronic charts that are put together using digital information in layers

watch   *n.* 1. a period of several hours of duty or a shift. 2. A group that stands the same hours, e.g., the night watch or the day watch. 3. A group that stands watch in the same department, e.g., the deck watch or the engine room watch.

watchkeeping   includes the conduct and real-time navigation of the ship, steering, keeping a lookout, monitoring radio communications, and monitoring machinery (engine room watchkeeping)

waterline   1. the line where the surface of the water touches the ship's side. 2. Any of the various marks on the ship that indicate the minimum allowable *freeboard* for various conditions.

X-band radar   a *radar* that operates on a wavelength of around 1.2 inches (3 centimetres) and a frequency of around 9 GHz. It produces a radar picture that is more detailed and sharp than the *S-band radar* but is more affected by precipitation and by ocean waves. It is what the navigator will generally use until it has reached the limit of its ability to cope with heavy rain or seas.

INDEX

Page numbers in **bold** refer to illustrations; page numbers followed by "n" refer to a footnote (e.g., 87n14 refers to note 14 on page 87)

ABOUT THE AUTHOR

COLIN HENTHORNE WAS BORN IN VANCOUVER AND GREW UP IN British Columbia. He has spent nearly all his life living and working on the water. He got his first command at the age of twenty-one and his entire career has been dedicated to command. He sailed as a master with BC Ferries starting in 1990 and was fifty-two when the *Queen of the North* sank. He has continued to work aboard and to command ships. At the time of writing he is a Canadian Coast Guard Rescue Co-ordinator at the Joint Rescue Co-ordination Centre in Victoria, BC.